Air Fryer Cookbook with Pictures

*Quick & Easy Air Fryer Recipes
for Beginners and Advanced Users
to Cook Homemade Meals*

Full-Color Edition

Fresh Ideas

CECILY GOODWIN

DEDICATION

Thank you to all my lovely readers
who are holding my book in their hands!

Copyright © 2023 by Cecily Goodwin
ISBN: 9798857883303

All rights reserved.

No part of this book may be reproduced in any form or by any electronic or mechanical means except for a brief quotation embodied in articles or reviews without written permission from its publisher.

DISCLAIMER

The material and recipes contained in this book are provided for informational purposes only. Please consult a qualified healthcare provider before changing your diet or lifestyle. The author does not assume any liability or responsibility to anyone for using all or any information in this book concerning any loss or damage caused or alleged to be caused directly or indirectly by the provided information.

All images are from depositphotos.com.

CONTENTS

Introduction 4
How Does the Air Fryer Work?............. 5
Benefits of Using.................................. 5
Air Fryer Cooking Techniques 7
Tips & Tricks 7
Air Fryer Conversion............................ 9
Air Fryer Cooking Chart 10
Air Fryer Recipes 12
Breakfast 13
- Cheesy Chicken Sandwich 13
- French Toast Sticks............................. 14
- Fluffy Pancakes 15
- Cheese & Ham Egg Rolls..................... 16
- Avocado Toast 17
- Breakfast Bombs 18
- Avocado Eggs 19
- Hard Boiled Eggs 20
- Egg Bites 21
- Breakfast Burritos 22
- Egg-Bacon Cups 23
- English Muffin Pizza 24
- Granola...25
- Quesadillas 26

Poultry...27
- Chicken Empanadas............................27
- Firecracker Chicken 28
- Chicken Bombs 29
- Mustard Honey Chicken Wings........... 30
- Almond Crusted Chicken 31
- Greek Chicken Burger 32
- Green Chicken Enchiladas................... 33
- Honey Garlic Wings 34
- Breaded Chicken Tenders....................35
- BBQ Chicken Wings 36
- Chicken Stuffed Peppers 37
- Jamaican Jerk Chicken 38
- Flavorful Chicken Breasts................... 39
- Stuffed Chicken Breasts 40
- Turkey Meatballs............................... 41
- Crispy Bone-in Chicken 42
- Fried Turkey Crown 43
- Roasted Turkey Legs.......................... 44
- Breaded Bone-in Chicken 45

Beef & Pork 46
- Hamburger.. 46
- Bacon Wrapped Sausages 47
- Juicy Steak 48
- Egg Rolls 49
- Bacon Wrapped Potatoes.................... 50
- Roasted Lamb Leg.............................. 51
- Meatballs..52
- Glazed Ham.......................................53
- Super Easy Meatloaf 54
- Fried Potato & Sausages 55
- Roast Pork...56
- Tender Pork Chops 57

Fish & Seafood 58
- Chimichurri Salmon............................ 58
- Salmon Burger 59

Coconut Shrimp 60
Fried Salmon......................................61
Bacon Wrapped Scallops 62
Crispy Fish Cake 63
Catfish Nuggets..................................64
Tuna Cakes...65
Breaded Fish Fillets.............................66
White Fish with Garlic 67
Vegetables....................................... 68
- Roasted Miso Asparagus..................... 68
- Korean Cauliflower Bites.....................69
- Spiced Bean Tacos 70
- Crispy Potato Skins 71
- Eggplant Parmesan Bites.....................72
- Garlic Mushrooms 73
- Roasted Parmesan Tomatoes 74
- Cabbage Steak...................................75
- Crispy Potato Wedges 76
- Spicy French Fries..............................77
- Roasted Vegetables............................78
- Crispy Tofu 79
- Sweet Potato Fries............................. 80
- Roasted Butternut Squash 81
- Garlic Broccoli 82
- Zucchini Fritters 83
- Fried Spaghetti Squash 84
- Cheese-Bacon Fries............................85

Snacks & Bread 86
- Wonton Chips 86
- Roasted Garlic...................................87
- Popcorn Shrimp 88
- Nachos... 89
- Pizza Rolls 90
- Fried Calamari 91
- Stuffed Mushrooms 92
- Pizza Bagels......................................93
- Fried Cheese Sticks............................94
- Banana Chips 95
- Apple Chips 96
- Bacon-Wrapped Dates 97

Desserts 98
- Bananas 98
- Apple Galette.....................................99
- Easy Donuts 100
- Quick Scones 101
- Cupcakes 102
- Apple Fritters 103
- Baked Apples....................................104
- Bread Pudding 105
- Nutella Cookies 106
- Caramelized Peaches 107
- Monkey Bread...................................108
- Carrot Cake 109
- Banana Cake..................................... 110
- Blueberry Crisp 111
- Brownies..112

Conclusion 113
Leave Your Review........................113
Recipe Index 114

INTRODUCTION

Welcome to the world of air fryers! Congratulations on your new purchase!

The air fryer has taken the culinary world by storm, revolutionizing the way we cook and enjoy our favorite foods. Its popularity stems from its ability to create deliciously crispy and flavorful dishes with significantly less oil than traditional frying methods. With its innovative technology, the air fryer circulates hot air around the food, leading to a golden and crispy exterior while maintaining moist and tender interiors.

I have found myself a bit addicted to cooking via air fryer because of the delicious taste of every food at the end. As an avid enthusiast of this great kitchen appliance, this marks my cookbook dedicated to the wonders of air frying. I have delved deep into the realm of air frying, experimenting with ingredients, techniques, and flavors to bring you a collection of exciting recipes that will tantalize your taste buds and enlarge your culinary repertoire. In this book, you will find a treasure trove of tested and foolproof recipes specially crafted for your air fryer.

Within these pages, you will discover various dishes starting from appetizers to main courses and even delectable desserts. Each recipe has been carefully developed, tested, and perfected to ensure exceptional results whenever you fire your air fryer. Prepare to be amazed as you explore fresh ideas, embrace new tastes, and unlock the full potential of your air fryer.

I am thrilled to share these culinary creations that have brought me joy and satisfaction. I sincerely hope this cookbook will inspire and empower you to embark on air-frying adventures. Prepare to embark on a flavorful journey and let the air fryer work its magic as we dive into the exciting world of delicious and healthier cooking.

Let's go!

air fryer

HOW DOES THE AIR FRYER WORK?

The way air fryers work is easy to understand. The hot air circulates the food you place inside. As with any other cooking process, a chemical reaction called the Maillard effect manages the food's colorful look and amazing flavor.

Heated air in the fryer comprises fine oil droplets that remove the food's moisture. Interestingly, you don't need to add much oil for a successful cooking process. You can use only one tablespoon and get crispy traditional fried food that tastes delicious at the same time.

As a result, you can have food that doesn't contain unhealthy fat and calories. You will be also pleasantly surprised to see the similarity of the fried food taste.

BENEFITS OF USING

I want to highlight briefly the main Air Fryer benefits.

Ease of use

Air fryers are simple. They

don't have many moving parts or buttons on them. It is pretty much like a traditional oven.

Everything you need to do is to:
1. Set the cooking temperature,
2. Set the cooking time,
3. Put your food inside the air fryer basket.

And wait for when it will be done. That's it!

Sometimes when you want to get a crispy cover from all sides, you may need to shake the basket or flip the food while cooking — no special movements.

When only the inner basket heats up during cooking (besides, it will cool down quickly), kids have less possibility to burn themselves, unlike they can do it on the oven or stove.

Healthy way of cooking

Air frying is healthier than traditional deep frying. The main reason is that it requires little to no oil but can brown and crisp your food as traditional fryers do.

Only a small amount of oil is needed to achieve excellent results in the air fryer. The oil used in the air fryer is effectively utilized, while any excess oil drains away from the food. It makes the air fryer a perfect cooking appliance for various dishes like mozzarella sticks, French fries, fried pickles, fried fish, chicken nuggets, and many more. You can enjoy the same crispness without the additional saturated fats typically associated with deep-frying in oil.

Cooking Efficiency

Spend half less time in the kitchen! Air fryers will heat quickly and keep the heat inside throughout cooking. This feature will help to cook the food faster than in a stove top or oven.

You will also evaluate a fast clean-up process. Most air fryers have removable baskets that can be easily wiped down, washed, and cleaned.

Versatility

You can cook your food using different cooking methods: baking, grilling, roasting, reheating, steaming, stir-frying, broiling, and, of course, frying. So traditional fried food is not the only one you can prepare using this amazing appliance. Look at this wider. Baked chicken breast will leave moist inside and crispy outside, as you have just removed it from the grill.

Air fryers are vegan, veggie, and vegetarian-lover friendly too. Spritz some of your favorite vegetables, such as Brussels sprouts or asparagus, with a touch of oil, and "fry" them in the air fryer until they reach crispy perfection! This convenient method makes meal-prepping vegetables a breeze.

The French fries aren't the only chip you can prepare. Try making delightful kale or sweet potato chips with a "frying" technique!

You'll be surprised you can even prepare delectable desserts using an air fryer. You can find some of them at the end of this book.

AIR FRYER COOKING TECHNIQUES

Air fryers can offer you to prepare food using different cooking techniques that can ultimately change the taste. So here are the most popular air fryer cooking techniques you can try:

• *Frying*. It's a great alternative to the deep-frying process as it uses hot air and just 1 tablespoon of oil to get golden-brown, crispy food.

• *Baking*. The air fryer can also bake various dishes, such as cakes, bread, and even desserts,

by just circulating hot air around the food.

• *Grilling*. The air fryer can grill various vegetables, fish, or meat for that delicious charred flavor. Remember to use a grill basket or pan while cooking.

• *Roasting*. The air fryer can help you roast vegetables, meat, or nuts, ensuring enhanced flavor and a crispy texture.

TIPS & TRICKS

Let me share with you useful tips & tricks for each air fryer technique.

Frying:

• If you want a crispy texture, spread cooking spray or a thin layer of oil over the food.

• Preheat your air fryer to 400°F before frying and flip halfway through.

• Shake the basket while cooking to cook the food evenly.

Baking:

• Preheat your air fryer to 325°F before baking, and check the readiness occasionally.

• Use the baking pan accessory for cooking muffins, cakes, and other desserts.

• If you want to check the doneness, use the toothpick by inserting it in the center of baked goods.

Grilling:

- Preheat your air fryer to 400°F before grilling, flipping halfway through, and check the readiness occasionally.
- Use the grill pan for grilling seafood, vegetables, and meat.
- Brush the prepared food with some oil to get a crispy cover and prevent it from sticking.

Roasting:

- Spread the prepared food in a single layer on the air fryer tray or basket to roast it evenly.
- Preheat your air fryer to 375°F before roasting, flipping halfway through, and check the readiness occasionally.
- If you want to check the doneness, use the thermometer by inserting it in the center of the meat to check the internal temperature.

Q&A

What if my air fryer is different from the one on the book cover?

Air fryers can have different sizes or shapes and may vary in how the food is put inside, but they work similarly. I have tested my recipes in various models to ensure they can be cooked in every air fryer.

Not all air fryers feature removable drawers; certain models have top-loading mechanisms without a drawer. It's crucial to refer to your air fryer's instruction manual to determine whether the drawer is removable. Some air fryers have tiered racks instead of a basket. In such cases, you can prepare all of my recipes using the bottom rack for cooking.

Some air fryer brands also offer extra-large (XL) sizes with a larger drawer capacity. While recipes from this book are compatible with XL air fryers, they were specifically designed with standard-size air fryers in mind, making an XL model unnecessary for their execution.

How to choose the right cooking time and temperature for your air fryer model?

While settings can differ among different air fryers, I tested recipes from this book in multiple models and want to ask you to test them too. Here are some useful pieces of advice to follow.

Cooking time: I recommend consistently verifying the doneness of food at the low end of the time range and cooking longer as necessary. The specified cooking duration in a recipe accommodates minor variations among different models.

Cooking temperature: Various air fryers utilize different temperature increments, ranging from 10 to 30 degrees. If your air fryer lacks the exact temperature setting mentioned in the recipe, opt for the nearest available temperature setting.

How to maintain the air fryer after cooking?

It would be best if you cleaned the air fryer after every cooking. It includes wiping down the interior, cleaning the basket or tray properly, and checking the heating element for damage.

What should I do if I have any trouble with cooking?

Uneven cooking: If you encounter inconsistent cooking results, consider shaking the basket or flipping the food halfway through the designated cooking time. Another technique is reducing the amount of food in the basket to promote even airflow.

Smoke: In case excessive smoke is being emitted by your air fryer, ensure that the basket and tray are clean and not overloaded with food. Lowering the cooking temperature and reducing the

cooking time also help alleviate the issue.

Sticky residue: If you come across a sticky residue on the basket or tray, try soaking them in hot soapy water for a few minutes before gently scrubbing it with a non-abrasive sponge.

Odors: To address unpleasant smells emanating from your air fryer, clean the basket and tray thoroughly after each use. Additionally, placing a small bowl of vinegar in the air fryer and running it on a low temperature for a few minutes can aid in eliminating any lingering odors.

AIR FRYER CONVERSION

Don't become upset if you have found a delicious recipe cooked in the oven. You can make it in your air fryer. Just follow Mason's general rule of thumb.

You need to cut the cooking time by about 20% and simultaneously reduce the temperature by 25%. That is the only thing you need to do.

Please, pay attention to your food and check its readiness occasionally to avoid overcooking or burning. Flip the food halfway through if you want to get the crispy cover.

AIR FRYER COOKING CHART

VEGETABLES

	Temp (°F)	Time (min)		Temp (°F)	Time (min)
Asparagus (sliced 1-inch)	400°F	5	Mushrooms (sliced ¼-inch)	400°F	5
Beets (whole)	400°F	40	Onions (pearl)	400°F	10
Broccoli (florets)	400°F	6	**Parsnips** (½-inch chunks)	380°F	15
Brussels sprouts (halved)	380°F	15	Peppers (1-inch chunks)	400°F	15
Carrots (sliced ½ – inch)	380°F	15	**Potatoes** (small baby, 1.5 lbs)	400°F	15
Cauliflower (florets)	400°F	12	**Potatoes** (1-inch chunks)	400°F	12
Corn on the cob	390°F	6	**Potatoes** (baked whole)	400°F	40
Eggplant (1 ½-inch cubes)	400°F	15	**Squash** (½-inch chunks)	400°F	12
Fennel (quartered)	370°F	15	Sweet potato (baked)	380°F	30-35
Green beans	400°F	5	**Tomatoes** (halves)	350°F	10
Kale leaves	250°F	12	**Zucchini** (½-inch sticks)	400°F	12

CHICKEN

	Temp (°F)	Time (min)		Temp (°F)	Time (min)
Breasts, bone-in (1.25 lbs)	370°F	25	Legs, bone-in (1.75 lbs)	380°F	30
Breasts, boneless (4 oz.)	380°F	12	Wings (2 lbs.)	400°F	12
Drumsticks (2.5 lbs)	370°F	20	Game hen (halved – 2 lbs)	390°F	20
Thighs, bone-in (2 lbs)	380°F	22	Whole chicken	360°F	75
Thighs, boneless (1.5 lbs)	380°F	18-20	Tenders	360°F	8-10

BEEF

	Temp (°F)	Time (min)		Temp (°F)	Time (min)
Burger (4 oz.)	370°F	16-20	Meatballs (3-inch)	380°F	10
Filet mignon (8 oz.)	400°F	18	Ribeye, bone-in (1-inch, 8 oz.)	400°F	10-15
Flank steak (1.5 lbs)	400°F	12	Sirloin steaks (1-inch, 12 oz.)	400°F	9-14
London broil (2 lbs)	400°F	20-28	Beef Eye Round Roast (4 lbs.)	400°F	45-55
Meatballs (1-inch)	370°F	7			

PORK AND LAMB

	Temp (°F)	Time (min)		Temp (°F)	Time (min)
Loin (2 lbs.)	360°F	55	Bacon (thick cut)	400°F	6-10
Pork chops (1-inch, 6.5 oz.)	400°F	12	Sausages	380°F	15
Tenderloin	370°F	15	Lamb loin chops (1-inch thick)	400°F	8-12
Bacon (regular)	400°F	5-7	Rack of lamb (1.5 – 2 lbs.)	380°F	22

FISH AND SEAFOOD

	Temp (°F)	Time (min)		Temp (°F)	Time (min)
Calamari (8 oz.)	400°F	4	Tuna steak	400°F	7-10
Fish fillet (1-inch, 8 oz.)	400°F	10	Scallops	400°F	5-7
Salmon, fillet (6 oz.)	380°F	12	Shrimp	400°F	5
Swordfish steak	400°F	10	Crab cakes	400°F	10
Lobster tails	370°F	5-7			

CHEESY CHICKEN SANDWICH

Cooking Time: 20 Minutes   **Yield:** 2 Sandwiches

INGREDIENTS

- 4 slices of sandwich bread
- 4 slices of cheddar cheese
- 1 cup of cooked & shredded chicken
- ¼ cup of buffalo sauce
- 2 tablespoons of butter
- 1 teaspoon of ranch seasoning mix
- ¼ cup of crumbled blue cheese*

INSTRUCTIONS

1. Spread all butter over one side of each piece of bread and sprinkle over with spices.
2. Put 2 bread pieces in the air fryer, butter side down. Cover each piece with 1 slice of cheddar cheese.
3. Mix the cooked chicken with the buffalo sauce to combine evenly and divide in half.
4. Spread the chicken with the blue cheese* on top of the cheese and cover with the remaining cheese slices. Put the second bread piece on top, butter side up.
5. Air fryer the prepared sandwiches at 360°F for 4 minutes, flip them, and continue frying for 3-4 minutes until golden brown.
6. Serve** warm and enjoy your Cheesy Chicken Sandwich!

USEFUL NOTES

* If you don't like eating blue cheese, you can omit it.
** It tastes good with blue cheese or ranch for dipping.
If you want to use canned chicken, try to buy one that is low in sodium. Otherwise, your sandwiches will be too salty.
Per 1 Serving (1 Sandwich) - Calories: 526, Carbohydrates: 28 g, Fat: 34 g, Protein: 27 g, Sugar: 3 g, Sodium: 2542 mg, Cholesterol: 118 mg.

FRENCH TOAST STICKS

Cooking Time: 15 Minutes **Yield:** 2 Servings

INGREDIENTS

- 4 slices of wheat or gluten-free bread
- 1/3 cup of dairy or plant-based milk
- 2 large eggs
- 1 tablespoon of melted butter
- ¼ teaspoon of cinnamon
- ½ teaspoon of pure vanilla extract
- Maple syrup, for serving

INSTRUCTIONS

1. Preheat your air fryer to 375°F.
2. Whisk milk, eggs, butter, cinnamon, and vanilla until well blended. Pour it into a wide flat dish.
3. Cut each bread slice into 3-4 strips.
4. Put strips into the egg-milk mixture for 10 seconds and flip it to soak each side.
5. Put the soaked strips into the preheated air fryer basket; keep them from touching. It is recommended to cook in batches.
6. Air fry each batch at 375°F for 6 minutes until crispy on both sides. If not, flip on the other side and cook for 2-3 minutes more.
7. Serve warm with any fresh berries and maple syrup. Enjoy your French Toast Sticks!

USEFUL NOTES

You can make some extra strips and freeze them for another time. Let them rest to cool completely, and place them in a freezer bag. Remove the air and seal the bag. Reheat before serving at 400°F for 2 minutes.

Per 1 Serving (2 Slices) - Calories: 283, Carbohydrates: 29 g, Fat: 13 g, Protein: 12 g, Sugar: 4 g, Sodium: 467 mg, Cholesterol: 201 mg.

FLUFFY PANCAKES

Cooking Time: 40 Minutes   **Yield:** 16 Pancakes

INGREDIENTS

- 2 cups of buttermilk
- 2 cups of all-purpose flour
- 2 large eggs
- 2 tablespoons of sugar
- 2 tablespoons of melted butter
- 1 teaspoon of baking soda
- 1 teaspoon of vanilla extract
- 1 teaspoon of baking powder
- ¼ teaspoon of salt

INSTRUCTIONS

1. Stir the eggs, buttermilk, vanilla, and butter in a mixing bowl until combined.
2. Sift in the all-purpose flour, baking soda, baking powder, salt, and sugar. Gently combine the dry ingredients with the wet ones until smooth consistency. Leave the batter for 20 minutes.
3. Spray some oil or cooking spray inside the silicone molds. Put 1 small scoop of batter in each mold and place inside the air fryer.
4. Air fry them at 375°F for 5 minutes until slightly golden on the tops. Flip the pancakes using tongs. Continue frying for the next 4 minutes until golden.
5. Repeat the previous 2 steps with the remaining batter. Make sure to grease the molds before cooking.
6. Serve warm with any fresh berries and maple syrup. Enjoy your Fluffy Pancakes!

USEFUL NOTES

Keep the leftovers in a sealed food container in the fridge for up to 3 days. Just reheat it in the air fryer for 20-25 seconds before serving.
You can freeze it, divided by parchment paper, for up to 3 months.
Per 1 Serving (1 Pancake) - Calories: 103, Carbohydrates: 15 g, Fat: 3 g, Protein: 3 g, Sugar: 3 g, Sodium: 156 mg, Cholesterol: 28 mg.

CHEESE & HAM EGG ROLLS

Cooking Time: 30 Minutes   **Yield:** 16 Servings

INGREDIENTS

- 16 egg roll wrappers
- 12 large eggs
- 8 ounces of diced ham
- ½ cup of shredded cheese
- Salt and ground black pepper, to taste

INSTRUCTIONS

1. Whisk eggs in a large skillet on medium heat. Add pepper and salt according to your taste. Cook, stirring frequently, until fully cooked. Add diced ham and cook for 1-2 minutes more. Stir in shredded cheese and take out from the heat.
2. Put 1/3 cup of the prepared mixture into an egg roll wrapper. To assemble the egg rolls, start by folding the bottom corner over the filling, followed by folding the side corners inwards, resembling the shape of an envelope. Proceed to roll it up tightly. To ensure a secure seal, lightly moisten the top corner with water before completing the rolling process. Repeat it for each egg roll.
3. Spray some oil or cooking spray inside the air fryer basket. Place 5-7 egg rolls into the basket, seam-side down, leaving some space between pieces. Air fry them at 400°F for 6-8 minutes until crispy.
4. Serve with your favorite sauce or salsa!

USEFUL NOTES

Per 1 Serving (1 Egg Roll) - Calories: 111, Carbohydrates: 8 g, Fat: 5 g, Protein: 9 g, Sugar: 1 g, Sodium: 328 mg.

AVOCADO TOAST

Cooking Time: 10 Minutes   **Yield:** 2 Servings

INGREDIENTS

- 2 slices of frozen bread
- 2 bacon strips*
- 1 avocado
- 1 tomato
- Lime juice, to taste

INSTRUCTIONS

1. Cut the bacon strips* in half and fry them in the air fryer basket at 400°F for 5-6 minutes.
2. Put 2 frozen bread slices in your basket. Lightly spread some oil over the bread. Toast them for 3 minutes at 380°F.
3. Mash up 1 avocado with a fork in a bowl. Add some lime juice to taste.
4. Cut the tomato into slices.
5. Arrange the toast with fried bread, avocado, tomato slices, and bacon strips on top.
6. Serve and enjoy your Avocado Toast!

USEFUL NOTES

* You can add air-fried sausages instead of bacon strips

Per 1 Serving (1 Toast) - Calories: 419, Carbohydrates: 24 g, Fat: 31 g, Protein: 14 g, Sugar: 3 g, Sodium: 499 mg.

BREAKFAST BOMBS

Cooking Time: 30 Minutes   **Yield:** 4 Servings

INGREDIENTS

- 1 can of biscuits
- 4 bacon strips
- 3 eggs
- 2/3 cup of shredded cheddar cheese
- 1 tablespoon of water

INSTRUCTIONS

1. Take 1 bread slice and put it inside the basket to absorb the excess grease. Spread the bacon on top and fry at 350°F for 10 minutes until crisp.
2. Scramble 2 eggs in a skillet on medium heat until cooked. Crumble bacon into the eggs and remove from the heat.
3. Take a biscuit and halve it. Shape one-half of the biscuit into a small bowl. Fill the bowl with a tablespoon of the bacon-egg mixture. Sprinkle cheese on top. Place the other half of the biscuit over the bowl, sealing the edges by pinching them together. Repeat it with all biscuits.
4. Whisk the remaining egg with 1 tablespoon of water in a small bowl.
5. Put parchment paper inside the basket and spray some oil. Spread breakfast bombs inside, leaving space between pieces. Lightly brush them with egg wash.
6. Air fry them at 320°F for 10-12 minutes, flipping hallway, until golden brown.

USEFUL NOTES

Try it with different ingredients such as ham, sausage, or bell pepper.
Per 1 Serving - Calories: 239, Carbohydrates: 4 g, Fat: 19 g, Protein: 12 g.

AVOCADO EGGS

Cooking Time: 20 Minutes   **Yield:** 4 Servings

INGREDIENTS

- 4 eggs
- 2 avocados
- 2-4 slices of bread
- Salt and ground black pepper, to taste

INSTRUCTIONS

1. Cut 2 avocados in half lengthwise. Remove the pit by giving it a firm whack with your knife, then twist it to release it from the flesh. Carefully carve out a portion of the avocado flesh, creating a hollow space in the pit area to accommodate an egg, but not all the way to the skin of the avocado. Repeat it with all avocado halves.
2. Put the avocado halves inside the air fryer basket. Place the bread slices between avocados. Crack 1 egg into the cavity of each avocado half. Add some salt and ground black pepper, according to your taste.*
3. Air fry them at 370°F for 7-12 minutes until the eggs are cooked according to your liking.
4. Serve warm and enjoy your Avocado Eggs!

USEFUL NOTES

* Fill free to add any additional toppings or seasonings such as lime juice, onion powder, cumin, paprika, or Parmesan cheese.
Use a piece of parchment paper inside to make cleaning the basket easier.
Per 1 Serving - Calories: 262, Carbohydrates: 16 g, Fat: 20 g, Protein: 9 g, Sugar: 2 g, Sodium: 136 mg.

HARD BOILED EGGS

Cooking Time: 22 Minutes   **Yield:** 2 Servings

INGREDIENTS

- 4 eggs

INSTRUCTIONS

1. Preheat your air fryer to 250°F.
2. Put your eggs into the preheated air fryer basket. Cook them for 13 minutes to get soft-boiled eggs, or 17 minutes to get hard-boiled eggs. But time can vary between different air fryer models.
3. Remove the eggs from the basket and put them into an ice bath.
4. Peel and serve. Enjoy your Hard Boiled Eggs!

USEFUL NOTES

You can keep them cooked in a fridge for up to 1 week.
You can freeze only cooked egg yolks. Remove them from the eggs and store the egg yolks in a container or freezer bag in the freezer for up to 3 months.
Per 1 Serving - Calories: 126, Carbohydrates: 1 g, Fat: 8 g, Protein: 11 g, Sugar: 1 g, Sodium: 125 mg, Cholesterol: 327 mg.

EGG BITES

Cooking Time: 25 Minutes **Yield:** 7 Servings

INGREDIENTS

- 7 eggs
- 4 chopped slices of bacon
- ¼ cup of shredded cheddar cheese
- 2 sliced green onions
- 1 tablespoon of heavy cream
- 1 tablespoon of milk
- ¼ teaspoon of mustard powder
- Salt and ground black pepper, to taste

INSTRUCTIONS

1. Preheat your air fryer to 340°F.
2. Whisk heavy cream, eggs, mustard powder, salt, and black pepper in a medium bowl until fluffy consistency.
3. Spray some oil inside the silicone molds, and divide chopped bacon, green onions, and cheese between the cups.
4. Transfer the molds inside the preheated basket and divide the egg mixture between cups.
5. Bake them at 340°F for 11-13 minutes until the eggs are set. Leave for 5 minutes before serving.
6. Serve warm and enjoy your Egg Bites!

USEFUL NOTES

Avoid adding too many mix-ins because these egg bites will not hold together.
Eggs will continue cooking after removing from the basket, so do not overcook.
You can keep the leftover in a container or zipper bag in a fridge for up to 7 days. Just reheat before serving for 4 minutes.
Per 1 Serving (1 Egg Bite) - Calories: 134, Carbohydrates: 1 g, Fat: 11 g, Protein: 8 g, Sugar: 1 g, Sodium: 172 mg, Cholesterol: 176 mg.

BREAKFAST BURRITOS

Cooking Time: 35 Minutes **Yield:** 6 Burritos

INGREDIENTS

- 6 flour tortillas
- ½ pound of raw breakfast sausage
- 4 eggs
- 1 medium potato
- 1 cup of shredded cheddar cheese
- ¼ cup of milk
- 1 tablespoon of oil
- 1 teaspoon of salt
- ½ teaspoon of ground black pepper

INSTRUCTIONS

1. Preheat your air fryer to 400°F.
2. Cut the peeled potato into ½" cubes and coat it with oil, pepper, and salt. Put in the preheated basket, fry at 400°F for 8 minutes, and set aside.
3. Cook the sausage in a skillet on medium heat until cooked. Remove from the skillet, leaving the grease inside the pan.
4. Whisk the milk, egg, a little pepper, and salt in a bowl. Pour it into a hot skillet with the grease. Scramble the eggs until fluffy.
5. Mix the fried potato cubes, scrambled eggs, shredded cheese, and cooked sausage in a bowl. Divide it between 6 tortillas and wrap them closed, using toothpicks.
6. Spray some oil over the burritos and transfer them into the basket. Fry them at 380°F for 7-8 minutes, flipping and adding oil halfway through cooking.
7. Serve warm with your favorite sauce!*

USEFUL NOTES

* It tastes good with salsa, sour cream, or hot sauce.
Experiment with bacon, avocado, bell pepper, or chopped onion.
Per 1 Serving - Calories: 484, Carbohydrates: 37 g, Fat: 27 g, Protein: 22 g.

EGG-BACON CUPS

Cooking Time: 20 Minutes   **Yield:** 6 Servings

INGREDIENTS

- 6 large eggs
- 3 slices of bacon
- ½ diced bell pepper
- Salt and ground black pepper, to taste

INSTRUCTIONS

1. Cut the bacon strips in half lengthwise. Place one half-slice of bacon on each silicone baking cup, ensuring it covers the surface of the cup.*
2. Gently crack an egg inside each cup, using the bacon as a base for the runny egg.
3. Sprinkle the tops with diced bell pepper, salt, and pepper to satisfy your taste buds.
4. Put the cups inside the air fryer basket. Carefully close the basket, ensuring that none of the cups topple over. Bake them at 330°F for about 10 minutes (the cooking time can vary based on how you like eggs). For getting over-medium eggs, you can start with 8 minutes; for over-well consistency, it will take 10 minutes. Remove the baked cups very carefully; they will be too hot.
5. Serve warm and enjoy Egg-Bacon Cups!

USEFUL NOTES

* If you want to get crispier bacon, pre-cook bacon to medium-rare before lining it inside cups.
Keep the leftovers in an airtight food container in a fridge for up to 4 days.
Per 1 Serving (1 Cup) - Calories: 115, Carbohydrates: 0 g, Fat: 9 g, Protein: 8 g, Sugar: 0 g, Sodium: 160 mg, Cholesterol: 10 mg.

ENGLISH MUFFIN PIZZA

Cooking Time: 10 Minutes   **Yield:** 3 Servings

INGREDIENTS

- 3 English muffins (split into halves)
- 1/3 cup of marinara sauce
- 3-4 chopped slices of pepperoni
- ½ cup of mozzarella cheese
- ½ teaspoon of dried oregano

INSTRUCTIONS

1. Preheat your air fryer to 400°F.
2. Spread marinara sauce over the cut side of each English muffin half. Add chopped pepperoni and cheese on top, and sprinkle over dried oregano.
3. Put them inside the preheated air fryer basket. Air fry the pizzas at 400°F for 4-5 minutes until slightly golden brown.
4. Serve warm and enjoy your English Muffin Pizza!

USEFUL NOTES

You can keep the leftovers in an airtight food container in a fridge for up to 3 days. Just reheat before serving.
Per 1 Serving (2 Halves) - Calories: 204, Carbohydrates: 29 g, Fat: 6 g, Protein: 8.6 g, Sugar: 4.5 g, Sodium: 506 mg, Cholesterol: 11 mg.

GRANOLA

Cooking Time: 20 Minutes   **Yield:** 8 Servings

INGREDIENTS

- 2 cups of old-fashioned oats
- ½ cup of raisins
- ½ cup of walnuts
- 3 tablespoons of brown sugar
- 3 tablespoons of coconut oil*
- 2 tablespoons of maple syrup
- ½ teaspoon of salt
- ½ tablespoon of cinnamon

INSTRUCTIONS

1. Cover the inside of the air fryer basket with parchment paper.
2. Mix oats, cinnamon, salt, and brown sugar in a large bowl. Pour in maple syrup with oil* and stir until the oats are fully covered.
3. Transfer the prepared mixture to the lined basket and spread it evenly inside. Fry it at 300°F for 15 minutes, stirring every 5 minutes. When 5 minutes are remaining, add in the walnuts.
4. After 15 minutes of cooking, remove the granola from the basket and spread it on a baking sheet in a single layer. Let it cool for 10 minutes, and stir in the raisins.
5. Serve warm and enjoy your Granola!

USEFUL NOTES

* You can add any neutral-tasting oil instead of using coconut oil.
Make sure to line the basket with parchment paper; the oats will fall through instead.
Stirring the granola every 5 minutes is important to crisp it up evenly.
You can keep the leftovers in an airtight food container for up to 6 months.
Per 1 Serving - Calories: 184, Carbohydrates: 22 g, Fat: 10.5 g, Protein: 3.4 g, Sugar: 12 g, Sodium: 150 mg, Cholesterol: 0 mg.

QUESADILLAS

Cooking Time: 10 Minutes   **Yield:** 2 Servings

INGREDIENTS

- 2 flour tortillas
- ½ cup of shredded cheese
- 4 tablespoons of refried beans

INSTRUCTIONS

1. Lay a tortilla on a flat working surface and spread 2 tablespoons of refried beans over one half of the tortilla. Then sprinkle half of the cheese over the beans and fold the tortilla, making a filled semicircle. Repeat these steps with the remaining tortilla.
2. Put the filled tortillas into the air fryer basket and fry them at 350°F for 8 minutes until golden and crisp, flipping halfway through cooking.*
3. Serve warm** and enjoy your Quesadillas!

USEFUL NOTES

* If the tortillas have slightly lifted away from the fillings, gently press them down with a spatula to secure them.

** I recommend serving with guacamole, salsa, Greek yogurt, or sour cream.

You can keep the leftovers in an airtight food container in a fridge for up to 4 days. Just reheat before serving.

Per 1 Serving - Calories: 310, Carbohydrates: 32 g, Fat: 14 g, Protein: 13 g, Sugar: 0 g, Sodium: 544 mg, Cholesterol: 30 mg.

CHICKEN EMPANADAS

Cooking Time: 20 Minutes   **Yield:** 8 Servings

INGREDIENTS

Empanadas:
- 1 ½ cups of shredded cooked chicken
- 4 ounces of cream chee
- 2 refrigerated pie crust
- 1 cup of shredded cheddar
- ½ cup of salsa
- 2 garlic cloves
- 1 egg
- 1 teaspoon of onion powder
- 1 teaspoon of cumin
- 1 teaspoon of salt
- ½ teaspoon of chili powder

Avocado Crema:
- 1 ripe avocado
- 1 teaspoon of lime juice
- 2 tablespoons of sour cream
- Pinch of salt

INSTRUCTIONS

1. Mix the shredded chicken, onion powder, cumin, shredded cheddar, cream cheese, garlic, salsa, and salt in a large bowl.
2. Dust your work surface with flour and roll the pie crust into 12" circles. Cut out circles from the dough using a 4" cookie or biscuit cutter to get in a total of 16 circles.
3. Spoon the filling mixture into the dough center. Fold them over and crimp the dough edges with a fork.
4. Brush the dough top with the whisked egg and sprinkle over with chili powder.
5. Put the prepared empanadas into your air fryer in a single layer, leaving some space between pieces. Air fry each batch at 350°F for 7 minutes until golden crust.
6. Cook the avocado crema. Mash the avocado with a fork in a bowl. Stir in lime juice, salt, and sour cream until smooth.
7. Serve warm with the prepared avocado crema. Enjoy your Chicken Empanadas!

USEFUL NOTES

Per 1 Serving (2 Empanadas) - Calories: 563, Carbohydrates: 50 g, Fat: 33 g, Protein: 18 g, Sugar: 4 g, Sodium: 839 mg, Cholesterol: 72 mg.

FIRECRACKER CHICKEN

Cooking Time: 20 Minutes **Yield:** 4 Servings

INGREDIENTS

Chicken Meat:
- 1 ½ pounds of boneless & skinless chicken breasts
- 2 large eggs
- 1 cup of cornstarch
- 1 tablespoon of water
- 1 teaspoon of salt
- ½ teaspoon of ground black pepper

Firecracker Sauce:
- ¾ cup of brown sugar
- ½ cup of buffalo sauce
- 1 tablespoon of apple cider vinegar
- ¼ teaspoon of red pepper flakes*
- ¼ teaspoon of salt

INSTRUCTIONS

1. Cut the chicken breasts into bite-sized cubes. Dry them with a paper towel.
2. Mix the cornstarch, pepper, and salt in a shallow dish to combine. Whisk the eggs with water in a separate bowl.
3. First, coat each chicken piece with the cornstarch, dip it in the beaten eggs, then back into the cornstarch mixture.
4. Spray oil inside the basket. Spread the batch of chicken in a single layer and spray oil over them.
5. Air fry it at 380°F fo 10 minutes, flipping and adding oil halfway through cooking.
6. Add all ingredients for firecracker sauce to a small saucepan. Simmer it on low heat, frequently stirring, for about 5 minutes.
7. Remove the fried chicken from the basket and coat it with enough sauce.
8. Serve warm** with the prepared sauce for dipping. Enjoy your Firecracker Chicken!

USEFUL NOTES

* If you don't like spicy food, you can omit the red pepper flakes.
** It tastes good with cooked white rice and steamed broccoli.
Keep the leftovers in an airtight food container in a fridge for up to 3 days.
Per 1 Serving - Calories: 612, Carbohydrates: 64 g, Fat: 12 g, Protein: 58 g.

CHICKEN BOMBS

Cooking Time: 20 Minutes   **Yield:** 16 Bombs

INGREDIENTS

- 1 ½ cups of shredded cooked chicken
- 1 can (8 counts) of refrigerated biscuit dough
- 1/3 cup of shredded cheddar cheese
- 1/3 cup of wing sauce
- ¼ cup of melted butter
- 2 tablespoons of cream cheese
- 1 tablespoon of sour cream
- 1 ½ teaspoons of ranch seasoning

INSTRUCTIONS

1. Mix the chicken, cream cheese, wing sauce, sour cream, and cheddar in a large bowl.
2. Open the can of biscuits and separate each piece in half to get in 16 thin dough slices.
3. Spoon the filling mixture into the biscuit center. Fold them over, crimp the dough edges tightly, and roll them into a ball.
4. Transfer the prepared biscuit bites inside the basket, leaving some space between pieces. Stir the ranch seasoning and melted butter and spread them over the biscuit dough.
5. Air fry each batch at 350°F for 5-6 minutes** until golden brown,
6. Serve warm* and enjoy Chicken Bombs!

USEFUL NOTES

* Serve them with blue cheese or ranch dressing for dipping.
** The second batch will cook faster as the basket will be preheated.
If you want to use canned chicken, try to buy one that is low in sodium. Otherwise, your bombs will be too salty.
You can keep the leftovers in an airtight food container in a fridge for up to 4 days. Just reheat at 350°F for 3-4 minutes before serving.
Per 1 Serving (1 Bomb) - Calories: 168, Carbohydrates: 15 g, Fat: 9 g, Protein: 6 g, Sugar: 1 g, Sodium: 532 mg, Cholesterol: 21 mg.

MUSTARD HONEY CHICKEN WINGS

Cooking Time: 35 Minutes   **Yield:** 10 Pieces

INGREDIENTS

- 10 chicken wing sections
- 2 tablespoons of mayonnaise
- 2 teaspoons of honey
- 2 teaspoons of yellow mustard
- 1 teaspoon of white vinegar
- Pinch of ground black pepper

INSTRUCTIONS

1. Spray some oil inside the air fryer basket and spread the wings in a single layer. Spray some oil over the wings too.
2. Air fry them at 400°F for 30 minutes, flipping halfway through cooking.
3. Meantime, cook the sauce. Mix the mayonnaise, honey, mustard, vinegar, and black pepper in a bowl.
4. Toss the cooked wings in the prepared sauce before serving. Enjoy your Mustard Honey Chicken Wings!

USEFUL NOTES

You can use store-bought honey mustard sauce, but I like to prepare it myself.

You can keep the leftovers in an airtight food container in a fridge for up to 4 days. Just reheat at 350°F for 3 minutes before serving.

Per 1 Serving - Calories: 119, Carbohydrates: 0.6 g, Fat: 9 g, Protein: 9 g, Sugar: 0.6 g, Sodium: 49 mg, Cholesterol: 38 mg.

ALMOND CRUSTED CHICKEN

Cooking Time: 15 Minutes   **Yield:** 4 Servings

INGREDIENTS

- 2 large skinless and boneless chicken breasts
- ½ cup of chopped almonds
- ¼ cup of mayonnaise
- 2 tablespoons of Dijon mustard
- ¼ teaspoon of salt
- ¼ teaspoon of ground black pepper

INSTRUCTIONS

1. Preheat your air fryer to 375°F. Spray some oil inside the basket.
2. Slice each chicken breast horizontally, making two thin cutlets to cook them evenly. Sprinkle with pepper and salt.
3. Mix the Dijon mustard and mayonnaise in a small bowl. Spread it over one side of each chicken piece.
4. Chop the almonds finely using a food processor. Pulse for 8-10 times. Avoid turning to flour. Spread it over the mayo-mustard chicken side, pressing down.
5. Place the chicken pieces inside the preheated basket, laying the almond-crusted side down. Brush the other side with the mayo-mustard mixture and spoon it with the almonds.
6. Air fry them at 375°F for 9 minutes or until the internal temperature reaches 165°F. Serve warm and enjoy it!

USEFUL NOTES

You can keep the leftovers in an airtight food container in a fridge for up to 3 days. Just reheat at 350°F for 3-4 minutes before serving.

Per 1 Serving - Calories: 185, Carbohydrates: 7 g, Fat: 11 g, Protein: 116 g, Sugar: 2 g, Sodium: 407 mg, Cholesterol: 37 mg.

GREEK CHICKEN BURGER

Cooking Time: 25 Minutes   **Yield:** 5 Servings

INGREDIENTS

Patties:
- 1 pound of ground chicken
- ½ cup of crumbled feta cheese
- 10 ounces of frozen spinach
- 1 chopped yellow onion
- 2 minced garlic cloves
- 1 teaspoon of dried oregano
- 1 teaspoon of dried parsley
- 1 teaspoon of black pepper
- 1 teaspoon of salt
- 1 teaspoon of dried marjoram

Spread:
- ½ cup of cream cheese
- ¼ cup of feta cheese
- 1 minced garlic clove
- 1 tablespoon of lemon juice
- ½ teaspoon of black pepper

Burger:
- 5 burger buns
- 1 sliced tomato
- ½ sliced red onion
- Lettuce leaves

INSTRUCTIONS

1. Unfreeze the spinach, drain very well and chop.
2. Mix all ingredients for the burger patties in a large bowl. Form into 4-5 equal patties.
3. Spray some oil inside the air fryer basket. Transfer the prepared patties into the basket, leaving some space between them. Air fry them at 390°F for 4-5 minutes on each side until the internal temperature reaches 165°F.
4. Meantime, add all spread ingredients to a blender or food processor and blend until smooth.
5. Make burgers. Cut each bun in half, spoon some spread over the inner side of each half, put lettuce leaves, tomato with onion slices, and 1 cooked pattie.
6. Serve warm and enjoy your Greek Chicken Burger!

USEFUL NOTES

Per 1 Serving - Calories: 297, Carbohydrates: 9 g, Fat: 18 g, Protein: 25 g.

GREEN CHICKEN ENCHILADAS

Cooking Time: 20 Minutes   **Yield:** 20 Enchiladas

INGREDIENTS

- 20 corn tortillas
- 18 ounces of green enchilada sauce
- 3 cups of shredded chicken
- 2 cups of shredded cheese
- 8 ounces of cream cheese
- 4 ounces of canned hatch green chili

INSTRUCTIONS

1. Mix the chicken, chilies, cream cheese, and half of the shredded cheese in a bowl.
2. Take a shallow pan that can fit in your air fryer basket and spread a thin layer of sauce inside it. Wrap tortillas with 2 tablespoons of chicken mixture and put them over the sauce.
3. After filling the pan with enchiladas, evenly cover them with half the remaining sauce and cheese. Reserve the rest of the sauce and cheese for the second pan of enchiladas. Ensure the enchiladas are fully coated with sauce and cheese for a delicious finish.
4. Bake each batch at 400°F for 6-8 minutes until the cheese is melted.
5. Serve warm with chopped tomatoes. Enjoy your Green Chicken Enchilada!

USEFUL NOTES

You can make them ahead and keep in the refrigerator for up to 3 days. Just reheat at 375°F for 5-7 minutes before serving.
You can freeze these enchiladas on a baking sheet, put them in a plastic bag, and keep them in a freezer for up to 3 months.
Per 1 Serving (1 Enchilada) - Calories: 73, Carbohydrates: 1 g, Fat: 6 g, Protein: 3 g, Sugar: 1 g, Sodium: 106 mg, Cholesterol: 20 mg.

HONEY GARLIC WINGS

Cooking Time: 30 Minutes   **Yield:** 20 Pieces

INGREDIENTS

- 2 pounds of chicken wings
- 1/3 cup of honey
- 3 minced garlic cloves
- 3 tablespoons of soy sauce
- 1 tablespoon of baking powder
- 1 tablespoon of rice vinegar
- 3 teaspoons of water
- 2 teaspoons of cornstarch mix
- Salt and ground black pepper, to taste
- Chopped parsley, for garnishing

INSTRUCTIONS

1. Divide the chicken wings into wingettes and drumettes. Dry them with a paper towel. Sprinkle the chicken parts with some salt and pepper, and toss with baking powder.
2. Preheat your air fryer to 390°F. Spray some oil inside the basket.
3. Spread the wings inside the preheated basket in a single layer. Air fry them at 390°F for 10 minutes, flip and cook for another 5-7 minutes until crispy cover.
4. Meantime, add the honey, rice vinegar, tamari, and garlic in a small saucepan. Bring it to a boil, add cornstarch with water, and mix. Simmer and stir until thickened.
5. Once the wings are fried, transfer them to a large bowl, and coat with the sauce.
6. Serve warm with chopped parsley on top. Enjoy your Honey Garlic Wings!

USEFUL NOTES

You can keep the leftovers in the refrigerator for up to 4 days. Just reheat at 390°F for 3 minutes before serving.

Per 1 Serving (1 Wing) - Calories: 75, Carbohydrates: 5 g, Fat: 4 g, Protein: 5 g, Sugar: 5 g, Sodium: 170 mg, Cholesterol: 19 mg.

BREADED CHICKEN TENDERS

Cooking Time: 30 Minutes   **Yield:** 4 Servings

INGREDIENTS

- 1 ½ pounds of chicken tenders
- ½ cup of plain breadcrumbs
- ½ teaspoon of sea salt
- ¼ teaspoon of ground black pepper
- ¼ teaspoon of paprika
- ¼ teaspoon of garlic powder
- ¼ teaspoon of onion powder
- Pinch of cayenne pepper

INSTRUCTIONS

1. Rub the chicken tenders with some olive oil.
2. Combine the breadcrumbs, ground black pepper, sea salt, onion powder, paprika, garlic powder, and cayenne pepper in a shallow bowl.
3. Press each chicken piece into the breadcrumbs mixture and try to coat. Spray some oil over them repeatedly.
4. Preheat your air fryer to 390°F. Spray some oil inside the basket.
5. Put inside 3-4 tenders at once, leaving some space between pieces. Air fry them at 390°F for 3 minutes, flip and continue cooking for 3 minutes more. Remove the meat and cook another batch.
6. Serve warm* and enjoy your Breaded Chicken Tenders!

USEFUL NOTES

* It tastes good with barbecue sauce and ranch dressing.
You can keep the leftovers in the refrigerator for up to 3 days. Just reheat at 390°F for 2-3 minutes before serving.
Per 1 Serving (3 Tenders) - Calories: 75, Carbohydrates: 10 g, Fat: 1 g, Protein: 6 g, Sugar: 1 g, Sodium: 357 mg, Cholesterol: 12 mg.

BBQ CHICKEN WINGS

Cooking Time: 35 Minutes   **Yield:** 5 Servings

INGREDIENTS

- 2 pounds of chicken wings
- 1 cup of BBQ sauce*
- 4 teaspoons of baking powder
- 2 teaspoons of smoked paprika
- 2 teaspoons of garlic powder
- 2 teaspoons of Italian seasoning
- 1 teaspoon of dried thyme
- 1 teaspoon of onion powder
- ½ teaspoon of sea salt
- ¼ teaspoon of ground black pepper

INSTRUCTIONS

1. Wash and dry the chicken wings with a paper towel. Divide them into wingettes and drumettes. Toss the chicken pieces with baking powder and seasonings in a large bowl until well coated.
2. Preheat your air fryer to 380°F. Spray some oil inside the basket.
3. Spread the coated chicken in a single layer in the preheated basket. Air fry them at 380°F for 10 minutes, flip and continue cooking for 7-10 minutes more until they are no longer pink.
4. Transfer the cooked chicken wings to a large bowl and cook the next batches. Add 2/3 cup of BBQ sauce to the fried wings and mix until well coated.
5. Serve warm with extra sauce and enjoy your BBQ Chicken Wings!

USEFUL NOTES

* If you like them a bit sweet, add a 1/3 cup of honey to the BBQ sauce.
You can keep the leftovers in the refrigerator for up to 5 days. Just reheat at 370°F for 3-4 minutes before serving.
Per 1 Serving (6 Wings) - Calories: 387, Carbohydrates: 10 g, Fat: 23 g, Protein: 35 g, Sugar: 4 g, Sodium: 1079 mg, Cholesterol: 221 mg.

CHICKEN STUFFED PEPPERS

Cooking Time: 30 Minutes **Yield:** 3 Servings

INGREDIENTS

- 3 bell peppers
- ¾ cup of mozzarella cheese
- 1 cooked chicken breast
- ½ cup of cooked quinoa
- 3 ounces of pesto

INSTRUCTIONS

1. Shred the cooked chicken.
2. Wash the bell peppers, slice off the top stems, and remove the seeds and membranes from the inside. Cut each pepper in half lengthwise, resulting in a total of 6 bell pepper halves.
3. Mix the shredded chicken, pesto, quinoa, and ½ cup of mozzarella cheese in a large bowl.
4. Preheat your air fryer to 400°F. Spray some oil inside the basket.
5. Stuff each pepper half with the chicken-quinoa mixture and put them inside the basket.
6. Bake the stuffed peppers at 350°F for 7-10 minutes until tender. Add the remaining cheese on top of the peppers during the last 2 minutes of cooking.
7. Serve warm and enjoy your Chicken Stuffed Peppers!

USEFUL NOTES

You can keep the leftovers in the refrigerator for up to 4 days. Just reheat them at 350°F for 3-4 minutes before serving.

Per 1 Serving - Calories: 348, Carbohydrates: 17 g, Fat: 20 g, Protein: 26 g, Sugar: 6 g, Sodium: 535 mg.

JAMAICAN JERK CHICKEN

Cooking Time: 35 Minutes   **Yield:** 2 Servings

INGREDIENTS

- 1 large chicken breast
- 2 cups of chopped potatoes
- 1-2 bell peppers
- 1 small zucchini
- ½ red onion
- 2 tablespoons of brown sugar
- 1 tablespoon of ground allspice
- 1 tablespoon of dried thyme
- 1 tablespoon of garlic powder
- 1 teaspoon of ground black pepper
- 1 teaspoon of cinnamon
- 1 teaspoon of salt
- 1/8 teaspoon of cayenne powder

INSTRUCTIONS

1. Combine the brown sugar, allspice, dried thyme, garlic powder, black pepper, cinnamon, salt, and cayenne powder in a small bowl.
2. Mix the chopped potatoes with half of the seasonings until well-coated.
3. Put the potatoes inside the basket, spray some oil, and air fry at 380°F for 8-10 minutes until tender.
4. Meantime, cut the chicken, zucchini, onion, and bell peppers into bite-sized pieces. Mix them all together with some oil and the remaining seasonings.
5. Remove the cooked potatoes from the basket and put in the chicken with vegetables. Air fry it at 380°F for 10-15 minutes.
6. Serve warm and enjoy your Jamaican Jerk Chicken with Vegetables!

USEFUL NOTES

You can keep the leftovers in the refrigerator for up to 4 days. Just reheat them at 380°F for 3-4 minutes before serving.
Per 1 Serving - Calories: 481, Carbohydrates: 84 g, Fat: 5 g, Protein: 32 g, Sugar: 46 g, Sodium: 1322 mg.

FLAVORFUL CHICKEN BREASTS

Cooking Time: 1 Hour   **Yield:** 4 Servings

INGREDIENTS

- 4 (6 ounces each) chicken breasts
- 1 tablespoon of olive oil
- 2 teaspoons of paprika
- 1 teaspoon of salt
- 1 teaspoon of garlic powder
- ½ teaspoon of oregano
- ½ teaspoon of ground black pepper
- ½ teaspoon of onion powder

INSTRUCTIONS

1. Wash and dry the chicken with a paper towel.
2. Rub the chicken breasts with olive oil and seasoning. Let it marinate for at least 30 minutes or overnight.
3. Preheat your air fryer to 375°F.
4. Spread the coated chicken inside the preheated basket, leaving some space between pieces. Air fry them at 375°F for 8 minutes, flip and continue cooking for 4-7 minutes more.
5. Let them cool for at least 5 minutes before slicing.
6. Serve warm and enjoy your Flavorful Chicken Breasts!

USEFUL NOTES

If you make dry chicken, it means you overcook it. Cut the cooking time by 1-2 minutes.

You can also cook chicken thighs instead of chicken breasts. Just adjust the cooking time based on the size of your pieces.

You can keep the leftovers in the refrigerator for up to 3 days. Just reheat them at 375°F for 3 minutes before serving.

Per 1 Serving (1 Chicken Breast) - Calories: 119, Carbohydrates: 2 g, Fat: 5 g, Protein: 15 g, Sugar: 1 g, Sodium: 665 mg, Cholesterol: 45 mg.

STUFFED CHICKEN BREASTS

Cooking Time: 40 Minutes   **Yield:** 4 Servings

INGREDIENTS

- 4 (6 ounces each) chicken breasts
- 3 ounces of cream cheese
- 1 ½ cups of chopped fresh spinach
- 2 ounces of feta cheese
- 3 tablespoons of diced red bell pepper
- 1 minced garlic clove
- 1 tablespoon of olive oil
- ½ teaspoon of paprika
- ¼ teaspoon of dried oregano
- ¼ teaspoon of salt
- ¼ teaspoon of ground black pepper
- ¼ teaspoon of garlic powder

INSTRUCTIONS

1. Combine the cream cheese, feta cheese, garlic clove, spinach, bell pepper, and oregano in a bowl.
2. Lay the chicken breasts on a cutting board. To butterfly each chicken breast, make a lengthwise cut about ¾ of the way through the breast, ensuring not to cut all the way through.
3. Divide the prepared filling mixture between all chicken breasts, securing the pockets with toothpicks.
4. Preheat your air fryer to 360°F.
5. Rub the outside of the chicken breasts with oil and season them with garlic powder, paprika, pepper, and salt.
6. Put the chicken breasts in the preheated basket in a single layer. Air fry them at 360°F for 18-22 minutes until tender.
7. Serve and enjoy Stuffed Chicken Breasts!

USEFUL NOTES

Don't add extra salt to the filling mixture as the feta cheese is salty enough. You can keep the leftovers in the refrigerator for up to 2 days. Just reheat them at 360°F for 3-4 minutes before serving.

Per 1 Serving (1 Chicken Breast) - Calories: 274, Carbohydrates: 2 g, Fat: 17 g, Protein: 28 g, Sugar: 1 g, Sodium: 509 mg, Cholesterol: 108 mg.

TURKEY MEATBALLS

Cooking Time: 20 Minutes   **Yield:** 6 Servings

INGREDIENTS

- 1 pound of ground turkey
- ½ cup of seasoned breadcrumbs
- 1/3 cup of milk
- ¼ cup of grated Parmesan cheese
- 2 tablespoons of Worcestershire sauce
- 2 teaspoons of Italian seasoning
- 1 teaspoon of red pepper flakes *(optional)*
- ½ teaspoon of garlic salt

INSTRUCTIONS

1. Combine the ground turkey, breadcrumbs, milk, cheese, sauce, Italian seasoning, red pepper flakes*, and garlic salt in a large bowl.
2. Take about 1 ½ tablespoons of the meat mixture and roll using your palms to form 1" to 1 ½" meatballs.
3. Put the formed meatballs inside the basket, leaving some space between them.
4. Air fry each batch at 400°F for 10 minutes, flipping halfway through cooking.
5. Serve warm and enjoy your Turkey Meatballs!

USEFUL NOTES

* If you don't like spicy meatballs, you can omit the red pepper flakes.
You can also experiment with any other ground meat, like ground chicken, or that is a bit leaner than ground beef.
You can keep the leftovers in the refrigerator for up to 4 days. Just reheat them at 400°F for 3 minutes before serving.
Per 1 Serving - Calories: 172, Carbohydrates: 10 g, Fat: 5 g, Protein: 23 g, Sugar: 2 g, Sodium: 560 mg, Cholesterol: 50 mg.

CRISPY BONE-IN CHICKEN

Cooking Time: 1 Hour 15 Minutes   **Yield:** 4 Servings

INGREDIENTS

- 2 pounds of bone-in chicken
- 1 ½ cups of flour
- 1 ½ cups of buttermilk
- ¼ cup of hot sauce
- 2 tablespoons of cornmeal
- 1 ½ teaspoons of garlic powder
- 1 teaspoon of paprika
- 1 teaspoon of seasoned salt
- 1 teaspoon of ground black pepper
- 1/8 teaspoon of cayenne pepper
- Chopped green onion, for garnishing

INSTRUCTIONS

1. Preheat your air fryer to 370°F.
2. Mix the chicken, hot sauce, buttermilk, and ½ teaspoon of garlic powder in a bowl. Keep it in a refrigerator for at least 30 minutes.
3. Combine the flour, cornmeal, salt, paprika, black pepper, cayenne powder, and 1 teaspoon of garlic powder in a bowl.
4. Remove the chicken pieces from the marinade and dip into the flour mixture to coat evenly. Put them on a plate or pan and spray over with oil.
5. Put the coated chicken into the preheated basket in a single layer.* Air fry them at 370°F for 15 minutes. Spray oil on top, flip them, and continue cooking for 10-15 minutes more until crispy.
6. Serve warm with chopped green onion on top. Enjoy your Crispy Bone-in Chicken!

USEFUL NOTES

* Avoid overcrowding the basket to allow the air to circulate.
You can keep the leftovers in the refrigerator for up to 3 days. Just reheat them at 370°F for 3-4 minutes before serving.
Per 1 Serving - Calories: 500, Carbohydrates: 15 g, Fat: 33 g, Protein: 34 g, Sugar: 1 g, Sodium: 758 mg, Cholesterol: 191 mg.

FRIED TURKEY CROWN

Cooking Time: 50 Minutes   **Yield:** 6 Servings

INGREDIENTS

- 4 pounds of turkey crown
- 1 halved shallot
- 1 halved clementine
- 2 minced garlic cloves
- 1 teaspoon of dried mixed herbs
- 1 teaspoon of olive oil

INSTRUCTIONS

1. Preheat your air fryer to 360°F.
2. Dry the turkey with a paper towel and drizzle with olive oil.
3. Season the turkey crown well and sprinkle the dried herbs evenly over the skin, ensuring full coverage. If the crown size allows, stuff the cavity with halved clementines, shallots, garlic cloves, and sprigs of fresh herbs. However, if the crown is too small to accommodate stuffing, you can place these ingredients around the turkey crown in the air fryer basket instead. Regardless of the chosen method, make sure to put the turkey crown in the basket with the skin side down for optimal cooking.
4. Air fry it at 360°F for 30 minutes, turn it over, and continue cooking for 20-30 minutes more until the juices run clear when pierced with a knife in the thickest part of the meat. Cut it into slices.
5. Serve warm and enjoy it!

USEFUL NOTES

Per 1 Serving - Calories: 424, Carbohydrates: 11 g, Fat: 17 g, Protein: 57 g, Sugar: 10 g.

ROASTED TURKEY LEGS

Cooking Time: 45 Minutes **Yield:** 2 Servings

INGREDIENTS

- 2 large turkey legs
- 1 ½ teaspoons of smoked paprika
- 1 teaspoon of seasoned salt
- 1 teaspoon of brown sugar
- ½ teaspoon of garlic powder

INSTRUCTIONS

1. Mix the smoked paprika, garlic powder, seasoned salt, and brown sugar in a bowl.
2. Wash and dry the turkey legs with a paper towel. Rub them with the seasoning mixture to coat evenly.
3. Put the turkey inside the air fryer basket and lightly spray over with olive oil.
4. Roast it at 400°F for 20 minutes, flip the turkey legs, and continue cooking for 20 minutes more.
5. Serve warm and enjoy your Roasted Turkey Legs!

USEFUL NOTES

You can keep the leftovers in the refrigerator for up to 4 days. Just reheat them at 360°F for 5 minutes before serving.

Per 1 Serving - Calories: 988, Carbohydrates: 3 g, Fat: 46 g, Protein: 133 g, Sugar: 2 g.

BREADED BONE-IN CHICKEN

Cooking Time: 25 Minutes   **Yield:** 8 Servings

INGREDIENTS

- 2 pounds of bone-in chicken pieces
- 1 cup of flour
- 1 cup of buttermilk
- ½ cup of cornstarch
- 2 teaspoons of salt
- 1 teaspoon of smoked paprika
- 1 teaspoon of ground black pepper

INSTRUCTIONS

1. Preheat your air fryer to 350°F. Spray some oil inside the basket.
2. Combine the chicken, 1 teaspoon of salt, buttermilk, and ½ teaspoon of pepper in a mixing bowl. Marinate for 10 minutes.
3. Meantime, mix the flour, 1 teaspoon of salt, cornstarch, and ½ teaspoon of black pepper in a separate bowl.
4. Using a pair of tongs, carefully lift chicken pieces from the buttermilk, allowing excess liquid to drip off. Dip the chicken into the breading mixture to coat both sides evenly, and transfer to a plate. Repeat it with the remaining meat.
5. Put the chicken pieces inside the preheated basket in a single layer. Air fry them at 350°F for 15 minutes, flip and spray over oil, and continue cooking for 10 minutes more. Serve warm and enjoy it!

USEFUL NOTES

You can keep the leftovers in the refrigerator for up to 3 days. Just reheat them at 350°F for 5 minutes before serving.

You can keep the cooked chicken also in a freezer for up to 6 months. Just reheat at 350°F for 8-10 minutes.

Per 1 Serving - Calories: 273, Carbohydrates: 21 g, Fat: 13 g, Protein: 17 g.

HAMBURGER

Cooking Time: 25 Minutes   **Yield:** 4 Hamburgers

INGREDIENTS

- 4 hamburger buns
- 1 pound of 80/20 ground beef
- ¼ cup of barbecue sauce (optional)
- ½ teaspoon of onion powder
- ½ teaspoon of ground black pepper
- ½ teaspoon of salt
- ¼ teaspoon of garlic powder
- Toppings as desired

INSTRUCTIONS

1. Mix the meat, garlic powder, onion powder, ground black pepper, and salt in a medium bowl.
2. Form the prepared mixture into 4 patties (½" thick). Brush them with barbecue sauce.
3. Preheat your air fryer to 370°F.
4. Spread the prepared patties inside the preheated basket in a single layer. Air fry them at 370°F for 6 minutes, flip them and continue cooking for 3-5 minutes.
5. Serve on buns with desired toppings. Enjoy your Hamburger!

USEFUL NOTES

You can make the patties ahead and keep them in the refrigerator for up to 3 days. Just reheat at 370°F for 3 minutes before serving.
You can freeze the uncooked patties on a baking sheet, put them in a plastic bag, and keep them in a freezer for up to 3 months. Cook them in the air fryer, just add 5 more minutes.
Per 1 Serving (1 Hamburger) - Calories: 365, Carbohydrates: 22 g, Fat: 19 g, Protein: 25 g, Sugar: 3 g, Sodium: 581 mg, Cholesterol: 77 mg.

BACON WRAPPED SAUSAGES

Cooking Time: 35 Minutes + 4 Hours   **Yield:** 40 Pieces

INGREDIENTS

- 2 packages (8 ounces each) of thawed fully cooked breakfast sausage links
- ¾ pound of bacon strips
- ½ cup + 2 tablespoons of packed brown sugar

INSTRUCTIONS

1. Cut sausages widthwise in half, and cut bacon strips in half too. Wrap each sausage half with a piece of bacon.
2. Transfer ½ cup of brown sugar to a shallow bowl. Roll each bacon-sausage in sugar and secure it with a toothpick. Put all of them in a large bowl and refrigerate for at least 4 hours or overnight.
3. Preheat your air fryer to 325°F.
4. Put the first batch of sausages inside the preheated basket, sprinkle over them 1 tablespoon of brown sugar, and air fry them at 325°F for 15-20 minutes, turning halfway through cooking, until crispy bacon.
5. Serve warm and enjoy your Bacon Wrapped Sausages!

USEFUL NOTES

You can keep the leftovers in an airtight food container in a fridge for up to 3-4 days. Just reheat them at 325°F for 2-3 minutes.
Per 1 Serving (1 Piece) - Calories: 74, Carbohydrates: 4 g, Fat: 6 g, Protein: 2 g, Sugar: 4 g, Sodium: 154 mg, Cholesterol: 9 mg.

JUICY STEAK

Cooking Time: 20 Minutes   **Yield:** 2 Servings

INGREDIENTS

- 2 steaks (about 1" thick)
- 2 tablespoons of steak butter*
- 1 tablespoon of melted salted butter
- 1 tablespoon of olive oil
- Steak seasoning, to taste

INSTRUCTIONS

1. Take the steaks out of the fridge for at least 30-40 minutes before cooking.
2. Preheat your air fryer to 400°F.
3. Drizzle the steaks with oil and rub them with melted butter.* Season generously on each side.
4. Put the steaks inside the preheated basket. Air fry them at 400°F for 8-12 minutes** until the desired doneness. Let them cool for 5 minutes before serving.
5. Serve warm with some butter on top. Enjoy your Juicy Steak!

USEFUL NOTES

* You can cook it yourself if you don't have special steak butter. Mix ¼ cup of salted butter, 1 tablespoon of chopped parsley, 1 minced garlic clove, and a pinch of smoked paprika.
** If you like medium rare steak, cook it for 8-9 minutes; for medium steak – 9-11 minutes; for medium well – 11-12 minutes.
You can store the cooked steak in an airtight food container in a fridge for up to 3 days. Brush on some melted butter and reheat it at 400°F for 3 minutes.
Per 1 Serving (1 Steak) - Calories: 582, Carbohydrates: 1 g, Fat: 5 g, Protein: 46 g, Sugar: 1 g, Sodium: 168 mg, Cholesterol: 153 mg.

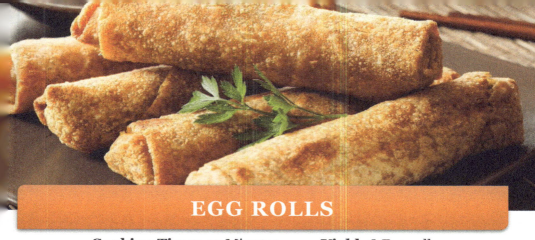

EGG ROLLS

Cooking Time: 40 Minutes   **Yield:** 8 Egg rolls

INGREDIENTS

- 8 egg roll wrappers
- 1 pound of ground pork
- 4 cups of fresh coleslaw
- 2 sliced green onions
- 2 minced garlic cloves
- 2 tablespoons of soy sauce
- 1 tablespoon of grated fresh ginger
- 1 tablespoon of flour

INSTRUCTIONS

1. Cook pork in a medium skillet until no pink remains. Add in ginger and garlic. Cook for 1 minute until fragrant. Add coleslaw and cook for 5-6 minutes. Stir in green onions and soy sauce. Remove from the heat.
2. Combine 1 tablespoon of flour with some water to make a paste.
3. Put 1 egg roll wrapper on your workplace and add 1/3 cup of filling in the center. Fold it diagonally, fold the sides in, and roll up, sealing the tip with the flour paste. Repeat it with the remaining egg roll wrappers. Rub the outside of each egg wrap with some oil.
4. Put the prepared egg rolls inside the basket. Air fry the rolls at 390°F for 8 minutes, flip, and cook for 3 minutes.
5. Serve warm with your favorite sauce. Enjoy your Egg Rolls!

USEFUL NOTES

You can keep the leftover in an airtight food container in a fridge for up to 3 days. Just reheat them at 400°F for 3 minutes.
Per 1 Serving (1 Egg Roll) - Calories: 203, Carbohydrates: 11 g, Fat: 12 g, Protein: 12 g, Sugar: 1 g, Sodium: 176 mg, Cholesterol: 42 mg.

BACON WRAPPED POTATOES

Cooking Time: 30 Minutes   **Yield:** 4 Servings

INGREDIENTS

- 1 pound of baby potatoes
- 16 bacon slices
- 1 tablespoon of olive oil
- ½ teaspoon of garlic powder
- ¼ teaspoon of salt
- Ground black pepper, to taste

INSTRUCTIONS

1. Soak some toothpicks in cold water.*
2. Cut the baby potatoes in half and put them in a large bowl. Add in the garlic powder, black pepper, salt, and oil. Mix to combine.
3. Preheat your air fryer to 400°F.
4. Cut the bacon strips in half widthwise. Take a piece of bacon and wrap it around the potato half. Secure it with a toothpick. Repeat it with the remaining bacon strips and potatoes.
5. Put the wrapped potatoes inside the preheated basket and air fry them at 400°F for 15-20 minutes until tender and crispy. I recommend cooking in 2 batches.
6. Serve warm and enjoy your Bacon Wrapped Potatoes!

USEFUL NOTES

* Soak the toothpicks in cold water for 5-10 minutes before using them. It will help to prevent them from burning.
You can keep the leftover in an airtight food container in a fridge for up to 2 days. Just reheat them at 400°F for 4-5 minutes.
Per 1 Serving - Calories: 303, Carbohydrates: 21 g, Fat: 21 g, Protein: 8 g, Sugar: 1 g, Sodium: 444 mg, Cholesterol: 29 mg.

ROASTED LAMB LEG

Cooking Time: 30 Minutes   **Yield:** 4 Servings

INGREDIENTS

- 4-5 medium potatoes
- 1.7 pounds of lamb leg roast
- 2 tablespoons of olive oil
- ½ tablespoon of parsley
- 1 teaspoon of thyme
- 1 teaspoon of oregano
- 1 teaspoon of paprika
- 1 teaspoon of garlic powder
- ½ teaspoon of ground black pepper

INSTRUCTIONS

1. Peel the potatoes, cut them into bite-sized pieces, and season with spices.
2. Put the lamb roast in the center of the basket and spread it around the potatoes. Drizzle over them with oil.
3. Roast it at 375°F for 15-20 minutes. Allow to cool for about 20 minutes before carving the meat.
4. Serve warm with mint jelly or your favorite sauce. Enjoy your Roasted Lamb Leg with Potatoes!

USEFUL NOTES

You can keep the leftovers in an airtight food container in a fridge for up to 4 days. Just reheat them at 375°F for 3-4 minutes.

Per 1 Serving - Calories: 776, Carbohydrates: 39 g, Fat: 52 g, Protein: 37 g, Sugar: 2 g, Sodium: 128 mg, Cholesterol: 141 mg.

MEATBALLS

Cooking Time: 30 Minutes   **Yield:** 16 Meatballs

INGREDIENTS

- 1 pound of lean ground beef
- ½ pound of lean ground pork
- 1 egg
- 1/3 cup of seasoned breadcrumbs
- 2 tablespoons of fresh parsley
- 2 tablespoons of milk
- 1 tablespoon of grated Parmesan cheese
- ½ teaspoon of onion powder
- ½ teaspoon of Italian seasoning
- ½ teaspoon of salt
- ¼ teaspoon of ground black pepper

INSTRUCTIONS

1. Mix the egg, breadcrumbs, parsley, milk, cheese, onion powder, salt, Italian seasoning, and black pepper in a medium bowl.
2. Add in pork and beef. Mix until well combined. Divide the prepared mixture into 16 equal meatballs.
3. Preheat your air fryer to 400°F.
4. Put the meatballs into the preheated basket in a single layer. Air fry them at 380°F for 12-14 minutes until browned. Let it cool for 3 minutes before serving.
5. Serve warm and enjoy your Meatballs!

USEFUL NOTES

You can keep the leftovers in an airtight food container in a fridge for up to 4 days. Just reheat them at 400°F for 3-4 minutes.
You can also keep the leftovers in a freezer for up to 1 month.
Per 1 Serving (1 Meatball) - Calories: 114, Carbohydrates: 2 g, Fat: 8 g, Protein: 9 g, Sugar: 1 g, Sodium: 143 mg, Cholesterol: 40 mg.

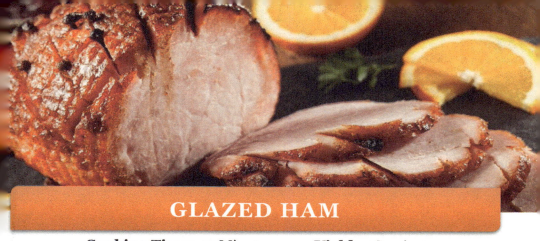

GLAZED HAM

Cooking Time: 40 Minutes   **Yield:** 4 Servings

INGREDIENTS

- 1 small (about 3 pounds) cooked ham
- 2 tablespoons of brown sugar
- 1 tablespoon of orange juice
- 1 tablespoon of honey
- 1 teaspoon of dry mustard

INSTRUCTIONS

1. Preheat your air fryer to 320°F.
2. Wrap the ham in foil, ensuring the end is at the top for easy opening.
3. Put the wrapped ham inside the preheated basket and air fry it at 320°F for 25 minutes.
4. Meantime, make a glaze. Combine the brown sugar, honey, orange juice, and dry mustard in a small bowl.
5. After 25 minutes of cooking, unwrap the meat and pour the glaze over the top. Continue cooking at 320°F for 10-15 minutes.
6. Close the foil and cook for 5-10 minutes more. Leave it to cool before serving.
7. Serve warm and enjoy your Glazed Ham!

USEFUL NOTES

A thinner flatter-shaped ham will be cooked quicker than a rounder football-shaped ham.
You can keep the leftovers in an airtight food container in a fridge for up to 3 days.
Per 1 Serving - Calories: 550, Carbohydrates: 11 g, Fat: 26 g, Protein: 64 g, Sugar: 11 g, Sodium: 3931 g, Cholesterol: 248 mg.

SUPER EASY MEATLOAF

Cooking Time: 45 Minutes   **Yield:** 4 Servings

INGREDIENTS

- 1 pound of lean ground beef
- 1/3 cup of seasoned breadcrumbs
- ¼ cup of tomato paste
- ¼ cup of diced onion
- ¼ cup of chili sauce
- ½ diced green bell pepper
- 1 egg yolk
- 1 minced garlic clove
- 2 tablespoons of grated armesan cheese
- 2 tablespoons of milk
- 1 tablespoon of chopped fresh parsley
- ½ teaspoon of Italian seasoning
- ¼ teaspoon of salt

INSTRUCTIONS

1. Preheat your air fryer to 350°F.
2. Mix the ground beef, bell pepper, breadcrumbs, onion, milk, cheese, parsley, garlic, egg yolk, salt, Italian seasoning, and black pepper in a large mixing bowl until well combined.
3. Divide the prepared mixture into 2 equal parts and form small meatloaves (2" wide and 5" long).
4. Air fry them at 350°F for 20 minutes.
5. Meantime, mix the tomato sauce with chili sauce in a small bowl.
6. Spoon the prepared mixture over the top of the meatloaves. Continue cooking at 350°F for 5-7 minutes.
7. Let it cool for 5 minutes before slicing.
8. Serve warm and enjoy your Super Easy Meatloaf!

USEFUL NOTES

Let the meatloaf rest for a while before slicing. It will help not to fall apart. You can store the leftovers in an airtight food container in a fridge for up to 4 days. Just reheat it at 350°F for 2-3 minutes before serving.

Per 1 Serving - Calories: 340, Carbohydrates: 14 g, Fat: 20 g, Protein: 25 g, Sugar: 4 g, Sodium: 709 mg, Cholesterol: 128 mg.

FRIED POTATO & SAUSAGES

Cooking Time: 40 Minutes   **Yield:** 4 Servings

INGREDIENTS

- ¾ pound of sliced smoked sausages
- 1 pound of peeled potatoes
- 1 sliced red bell pepper
- ½ cup of baby carrot
- ½ sliced white onion
- 2 minced garlic cloves
- 2 tablespoons of olive oil
- 1 teaspoon of lemon zest
- 1 teaspoon of lemon juice
- ½ teaspoon of salt
- ½ teaspoon of dried oregano
- ¼ teaspoon of ground black pepper

INSTRUCTIONS

1. Preheat your air fryer to 400°F.
2. Combine the garlic, lemon juice, lemon zest, olive oil, oregano, salt, and black pepper in a small bowl.
3. Cut the peeled potatoes into 1" wedges and mix them with half of the seasoning mix. Air fry them at 400°F for 12 minutes.
4. Toss the sliced sausages, bell pepper, onion, carrot, and the remaining seasoning. Open the air fryer and put it inside, shaking the basket. Continue air frying at 400°F for 5 minutes.
5. Serve warm and enjoy your Fried Potato & Sausages!

USEFUL NOTES

You can keep the leftovers in an airtight food container in a fridge for up to 5 days. Just reheat it at 400°F for 3-4 minutes before serving.

Per 1 Serving - Calories: 439, Carbohydrates: 27 g, Fat: 31 g, Protein: 14 g, Sugar: 3 g, Sodium: 1069 g, Cholesterol: 64 mg.

ROAST PORK

Cooking Time: 1 Hour 20 Minutes   **Yield:** 4-6 Servings

INGREDIENTS

- 3 pounds of roast pork leg*
- 1-2 tablespoons of coarse salt
- 1 tablespoon of olive oil

INSTRUCTIONS

1. Remove the roast from the packaging. Use paper towels to pat the roast dry, removing excess moisture. Take a small sharp knife and score the rind of the roast at 1 cm intervals. Be cautious not to cut into the meat while scoring.
2. Leave the meat uncovered in the refrigerator for at least 1 hour or overnight. It allows the surface of the meat to dry out, especially the rind, which is crucial for achieving crispy crackling.
3. Rub the meat with olive oil and salt, being sure to get into the scores.
4. Place it inside your air fryer basket and roast at 400°F for 20 minutes, then at 350°F until fully cooked (about 25 minutes for every 1 pound).
5. Let it cool for 10 minutes before slicing.
6. Serve and enjoy your Roast Pork!

USEFUL NOTES

Keep the leftovers in an airtight food container in a fridge for up to 5 days.
Per 1 Serving - Calories: 750, Carbohydrates: 0 g, Fat: 56 g, Protein: 58 g, Sugar: 9 g, Sodium:2496 g, Cholesterol: 225 mg.

TENDER PORK CHOPS

Cooking Time: 25 Minutes   **Yield:** 4 Servings

INGREDIENTS

- 4 (5 ounces) boneless pork chops
- ½ cup of grated Parmesan cheese
- 2 tablespoons of olive oil
- 1 teaspoon of dried parsley
- 1 teaspoon of sea salt
- 1 teaspoon of garlic powder
- 1 teaspoon of paprika
- ½ teaspoon of ground black pepper
- Slices of green onion, for garnishing

INSTRUCTIONS

1. Preheat your air fryer to 380°F.
2. Mix the cheese, garlic powder, paprika, black pepper, parsley, and salt in a shallow dish.
3. Rub each pork chop with olive oil. Coat every pork chop side with the cheese mixture.
4. Put 2 seasoned pork chops inside the preheated basket and air fry at 380°F for 10 minutes, flipping halfway through cooking.
5. Repeat the last step with the remaining pork chops.
6. Serve warm with some onion slices on top. Enjoy your Tender Pork Chops!

USEFUL NOTES

You can keep the leftovers in an airtight food container in a fridge for up to 3 days. Just reheat it at 380°F for 3-4 minutes before serving.
Per 1 Serving - Calories: 305, Carbohydrates: 2 g, Fat: 17 g, Protein: 35 g, Sugar: 0 g, Sodium: 685 g, Cholesterol: 90 mg.

CHIMICHURRI SALMON

Cooking Time: 25 Minutes **Yield:** 4 Servings

INGREDIENTS

- 2 pounds of salmon
- ½ cup of fresh cilantro leaves
- ½ cup of fresh basil leaves
- ½ cup of fresh parsley leaves
- 1 chopped medium shallot
- 3 chopped garlic cloves
- 1 tablespoon of lemon juice
- 1 tablespoon of red wine vinegar
- ½ teaspoon of salt
- ½ teaspoon of ground coriander
- 1 pinch of dried chili flakes *(optional)*
- ¼ cup of olive oil

INSTRUCTIONS

1. Mix the chopped garlic, shallots, vinegar, and lemon juice in a small bowl. Set aside.
2. Put the cilantro, parsley, basil, salt, and coriander into a food processor. Process all ingredients until finely chopped.
3. Add the shallot-garlic mixture along with the liquid to the food processor. Blend one more time until finely chopped.
4. While blending, slowly pour the olive oil until incorporated. The sauce should be slightly chunky. If you like spicy food, add in dried chili pepper flakes too. Transfer it to a small bowl.
5. Spray oil inside the air fryer basket. Brush both salmon sides with oil too. Place them inside the basket and fry at 390°F for 7-8 minutes or until the internal temperature of the fish fillet reaches 145°F.
6. Serve with lemon wedges and the chimichurri sauce on top. Enjoy it!!

USEFUL NOTES

Keep the leftovers in an airtight food container in a fridge for up to 3 days. You can freeze the prepared chimichurri sauce. Spread it between ice cube trays and freeze. Once frozen, keep them in a freezer bag for up to 6 months.
Per 1 Serving - Calories: 455, Carbohydrates: 3 g, Fat: 28 g, Protein: 46 g..

SALMON BURGER

Cooking Time: 1 Hour 35 Minutes   **Yield:** 4 Servings

INGREDIENTS

- 1 pound of salmon
- ¾ cup of panko breadcrumbs
- 2 tablespoons of Dijon mustard
- 2 tablespoons of chopped scallions
- 1 tablespoon of lemon juice
- 1 tablespoon of mayonnaise
- ¼ teaspoon of crushed red chili flakes
- Salt and ground black pepper, to taste
- 4 hamburger buns
- Toppings as desired

INSTRUCTIONS

1. Remove the skin and bones from the salmon fillets. Cut them into ¼" pieces. Take ¼ part of the pieces and put it in a food processor. Transfer the remaining part of the salmon to a large bowl.
2. Add lemon juice, mayonnaise, and mustard to a food processor. Pulse a couple of times until you get a thick paste. Transfer the prepared mixture to the remaining salmon pieces. Mix in scallions, bread crumbs, and chili flakes until well combined.
3. Form 4 even patties. Put them on a baking sheet, season with pepper and salt, and place in the freezer for 1 hour.
4. Preheat your air fryer to 400°F. Spray oil inside the basket. Put the patties into it. Air fry them at 400°F for 8 minutes, spray oil over and cook for 5 minutes more.
5. Make burgers from hamburger buns and with your favorite toppings. Enjoy it!

USEFUL NOTES

Store the patty leftovers in an airtight container in a fridge for up to 3 days.
Per 1 Serving (1 Patty) - Calories: 236, Carbohydrates: 9 g, Fat: 11 g, Protein: 24 g, Sugar: 1 g, Sodium: 240 g.

COCONUT SHRIMP

Cooking Time: 25 Minutes   **Yield:** 4 Servings

INGREDIENTS

- 1 pound of raw and peeled shrimp
- 2 large eggs
- ¾ cup of unsweetened shredded coconut
- ¼ cup of all-purpose flour
- ¼ cup of panko breadcrumbs
- ½ teaspoon of salt
- ½ teaspoon of garlic powder
- ¼ teaspoon of ground black pepper
- Lemon wedges, for serving

INSTRUCTIONS

1. Preheat your air fryer to 360°F. Spray some oil inside the air fryer basket.
2. Mix the garlic powder, flour, black pepper, and salt in a shallow bowl. Whisk the eggs in a second bowl. Combine the panko breadcrumbs with shredded coconut in a separate shallow bowl.
3. First, coat the peeled shrimps with the flour mixture, dip them into the beaten eggs, and then gently press them with the panko-coconut mixture.
4. Put the coated shrimp into the preheated basket, leaving some space between pieces. Spray some oil over the top. Air fry them at 360°F for 10-12 minutes, flipping halfway through cooking.
5. Serve warm* with lemon wedges. Enjoy your Coconut Shrimp!

USEFUL NOTES

* It tastes good with sweet chili sauce.
You can keep the leftovers in an airtight food container in a fridge for up to 3 days. Just reheat them at 360°F for 2-3 minutes.
Per 1 Serving - Calories: 304, Carbohydrates: 13 g, Fat: 15 g, Protein: 28 g, Sugar: 2 g, Sodium: 1237 g, Cholesterol: 368 mg.

FRIED SALMON

Cooking Time: 10 Minutes   **Yield:** 4 Servings

INGREDIENTS

- 4 salmon fillets (6 ounces each)
- 1 tablespoon of olive oil
- 1 teaspoon of garlic powder
- ½ teaspoon of paprika
- Salt and ground black pepper, to taste
- Tartar sauce, for serving
- Lemon wedges, for serving

INSTRUCTIONS

1. Preheat your air fryer to 400°F.
2. Rub each salmon fillet with oil and season with paprika, garlic powder, ground black pepper, and salt.
3. Put salmon fillets inside the preheated basket and air fry them at 400°F for 7-9 minutes.
4. Open the basket and check the doneness with a fork. You can cook for 1-2 minutes more if necessary.
5. Serve warm with lemon wedges. Enjoy your Fried Salmon!

USEFUL NOTES

It tastes good with cooked rice, barley, couscous, and a fresh salad.
You can keep the leftovers in an airtight food container in a fridge for up to 3 days. Just reheat them at 400°F for 2 minutes.
You can freeze the cooked salmon in an airtight food bag in a refrigerator for up to 3 months.
Per 1 Serving - Calories: 276, Carbohydrates: 1 g, Fat: 14 g, Protein: 34 g, Sugar: 1 g, Sodium: 75 g, Cholesterol: 94 mg.

BACON WRAPPED SCALLOPS

Cooking Time: 20 Minutes   **Yield:** 4 Servings

INGREDIENTS

- 12 large sea scallops
- 6 bacon slices*
- 1 minced garlic clove
- 1 tablespoon of melted butter
- 1 teaspoon of parsley
- ½ teaspoon of lemon pepper
- Salt and ground black pepper, to taste

INSTRUCTIONS

1. Soak short wooden skewers in water for 30 minutes.
2. Wash and dry scallions with paper towels. Season them with salt and ground black pepper according to your taste.
3. Cut each bacon strip in half widthwise to get 12 pieces. Wrap each scallop with the halved bacon strip and thread 3 scallops onto each skewer.
4. Mix the melted butter with garlic, lemon pepper, and parsley. Brush it over scallops.
5. Put the prepared scallops inside the air fryer basket and fry them at 350°F for 11-13 minutes until the scallops are cooked and the bacon is crispy.
6. Serve and enjoy Bacon Wrapped Scallops!

USEFUL NOTES

* If scallops are too large, take 1 bacon slice per scallop.
You can keep the leftovers in an airtight food container in a fridge for up to 3 days. Just reheat them at 350°F for 2 minutes.
You can also freeze the cooked scallops in an airtight food bag in a refrigerator for up to 3 months.
Per 1 Serving - Calories: 196, Carbohydrates: 2 g, Fat: 16 g, Protein: 10 g, Sugar: 1 g, Sodium: 420 g, Cholesterol: 40 mg.

CRISPY FISH CAKE

Cooking Time: 25 Minutes   **Yield:** 4 Servings

INGREDIENTS

- 12 ounces of chopped cod fillets
- 2/3 cup of pork rind panko breadcrumbs
- 1 egg
- 2 tablespoons of mayonnaise
- 2 tablespoons of sweet chili sauce
- 2 tablespoons of chopped fresh cilantro
- ¼ teaspoon of ground black pepper
- ¼ teaspoon of salt
- Lime wedges, for serving

INSTRUCTIONS

1. Preheat your air fryer to 400°F. Spray some oil inside the basket.
2. Put the chopped fish into a food processor* and blend until crumbly.
3. Mix the crumbled fish, cilantro, breadcrumbs, mayonnaise, egg, chili sauce, black pepper, and salt.
4. Form the prepared mixture into 4 patties.
5. Put these patties inside the preheated basket and spray some oil over them.
6. Air fry them at 400°F for 5 minutes, flip them, spray with oil, and continue cooking for 4-5 minutes until crispy and golden brown.
7. Serve warm with lime wedges. Enjoy your Crispy Fish Cake!

USEFUL NOTES

* If you don't have a food processor, chop the fish fillets until finely minced. You can keep the leftovers in an airtight food container in a fridge for up to 3 days. Just reheat them at 400°F for 2 minutes.

You can also freeze the cooked patties in an airtight food bag in a refrigerator for up to 4 months.

Per 1 Serving (1 Cake) - Calories: 176, Carbohydrates: 4 g, Fat: 8 g, Protein: 20 g, Sugar: 4 g, Sodium: 422 mg, Cholesterol: 85 mg.

CATFISH NUGGETS

Cooking Time: 30 Minutes   **Yield:** 4 Servings

INGREDIENTS

- 3 thawed catfish fillets
- 1 ½ cups of panko breadcrumbs
- ¾ cup of buttermilk
- 1/3 cup of all-purpose flour
- 1 large egg
- 3 tablespoons of water
- 1 teaspoon of salt
- ½ teaspoon of paprika
- ½ teaspoon of garlic powder
- ½ teaspoon of ground black pepper
- Lemon wedges, for serving

INSTRUCTIONS

1. Rinse and dry the catfish fillets. Cut them into 1" to 2" chunks, put them in a mixing bowl, pour in the buttermilk, and let it soak for 10-20 minutes at room temperature.
2. Whisk the egg with water in a shallow bowl. Mix the breadcrumbs, garlic powder, flour, paprika, black pepper, and salt in another bowl.
3. Drain off the liquid from the fish through a fine mesh strainer. Dip each chunk into the whisked egg, then coat with the breadcrumb mixture, shaking off any excess.
4. Preheat your air fryer to 400°F. Put the breaded pieces inside the preheated basket in a single layer. Spray some oil over them.
5. Air fry them at 400°F for 8 minutes, flipping halfway through cooking.
6. Serve warm with lemon wedges. Enjoy your Catfish Nuggets!

USEFUL NOTES

Per 1 Serving - Calories: 395, Carbohydrates: 41 g, Fat: 12 g, Protein: 30 g, Sugar: 5 g, Sodium: 845 mg, Cholesterol: 119 mg.

TUNA CAKES

Cooking Time: 25 Minutes   **Yield:** 12 Servings

INGREDIENTS

- 2 cans (12 ounces each) of chunk tuna in water
- ½ cup of seasoned breadcrumbs
- 2 eggs
- ½ diced white onion
- 4 tablespoons of mayonnaise
- 2 tablespoons of lemon juice
- ½ teaspoon of ground black pepper
- ½ teaspoon of salt

INSTRUCTIONS

1. Drain the tuna and transfer it to a mixing bowl. Add the eggs, breadcrumbs, mayonnaise, lemon juice, white onion, salt, and black pepper to the bowl. Mix it gently to combine.
2. Spray some oil inside the air fryer basket.
3. Shape this mixture into 12 patties. Put four of them inside the basket, leaving some space between pieces.
4. Air fry each batch at 375°F for 12 minutes, flipping halfway through cooking.* Cook another batch.
5. Serve warm with your favorite sauce. Enjoy your Tuna Cakes!

USEFUL NOTES

* If you want extra crispy patties, spray some oil on them after flipping.
You can store the leftovers in an airtight food container in a fridge for up to 3 days. Just reheat them at 375°F for 2-3 minutes.
You can also freeze the tuna cakes in an airtight food bag in a refrigerator for up to 3 months.
Per 1 Serving (1 Cake) - Calories: 83, Carbohydrates: 4 g, Fat: 5 g, Protein: 5 g, Sugar: 1 g, Sodium: 260 mg, Cholesterol: 39 mg.

BREADED FISH FILLETS

Cooking Time: 20 Minutes   **Yield:** 8 Servings

INGREDIENTS

- 8 defrost raw fish fillets
- 1 cup of dry bread crumbs
- 1 tablespoon of olive oil
- ½ teaspoon of paprika
- ½ teaspoon of salt
- ¼ teaspoon of onion powder
- ¼ teaspoon of chili powder
- ¼ teaspoon of garlic powder
- ¼ teaspoon of ground black pepper
- Lemon wedges, for serving
- Tartar sauce, for serving

INSTRUCTIONS

1. Wash and dry fish fillets with a paper towel. Coat them with olive oil.
2. Mix the chili powder, bread crumbs, paprika, black pepper, onion powder, salt, and garlic powder.
3. Coat each fillet with the breadcrumb mixture and put them inside your air fryer basket.
4. Air fry them at 390°F for 8 minutes, flip the fillets, and continue cooking for 4-7 minutes more.
5. Serve warm with lemon wedges and tartar sauce. Enjoy your Breaded Fish Fillets!

USEFUL NOTES

You can keep the leftovers in an airtight food container in a fridge for up to 4 days. Just reheat them at 390°F for 2-3 minutes.
Per 1 Serving (1 Fillet) - Calories: 153, Carbohydrates: 11 g, Fat: 3 g, Protein: 21 g, Sugar: 0 g, Sodium: 269 mg, Cholesterol: 50 mg.

WHITE FISH WITH GARLIC

Cooking Time: 15 Minutes   **Yield:** 2 Servings

INGREDIENTS

- 2 tilapia fillets (6 ounces each)
- ½ teaspoon of onion powder
- ½ teaspoon of lemon pepper seasoning
- ½ teaspoon of garlic powder
- Sea salt and ground black pepper, to taste
- Lemon wedges, for serving

INSTRUCTIONS

1. Preheat your air fryer to 360°F.* Spray some oil inside the basket.
2. Wash and dry fish fillets with a paper towel. Spray oil over them and season with onion powder, garlic powder, lemon pepper, black pepper, and salt.
3. Put the seasoned fillets inside the preheated basket. Add a few lemon wedges next to the fish.
4. Air fry them at 360°F for 6-12 minutes until a fork can easily flake the fillets.
5. Serve warm with lemon wedges. Enjoy your White Fish with Garlic!

USEFUL NOTES

* To avoid sticking, lay perforated air fryer baking paper inside the basket and spray over some oil.

You can keep the leftovers in an airtight food container in a fridge for up to 3 days. Just reheat them at 360°F for 2-3 minutes.

Per 1 Serving (1 Fillet) - Calories: 169, Carbohydrates: 1 g, Fat: 3 g, Protein: 34 g, Sugar: 1 g, Sodium: 89 mg, Cholesterol: 85 mg.

ROASTED MISO ASPARAGUS

Cooking Time: 15 Minutes   **Yield:** 4 Servings

INGREDIENTS

- 1 pound of asparagus spears
- 3 tablespoons and 1 teaspoon of olive oil
- 3 tablespoons of rice vinegar
- 1 tablespoon of sesame oil
- 1 tablespoon of white miso
- ½ tablespoon of honey
- ½ tablespoon of sesame seeds
- ¼ teaspoon of sea salt
- Extra sesame seeds, for garnishing

INSTRUCTIONS

1. Add the white miso, sesame oil, rice vinegar, honey, sea salt, sesame seeds, and 3 tablespoons of olive oil in a small jar. Cover it with a lid and make a good shake.
2. Wash and dry asparagus. Cut tough ends from the asparagus and toss the main part with 1 teaspoon of olive oil.
3. Preheat your air fryer to 360°F.
4. Place asparagus spears inside the preheated basket in a single layer. Roast them at 360°F for 5 minutes. Flip them with tongs and continue cooking for an extra 3-7 minutes, depending on the thickness of the asparagus. Sprinkle sesame seeds over the roasted asparagus.
5. Serve warm with the prepared miso-sesame dressing. Enjoy your Roasted Miso Asparagus!

USEFUL NOTES

You can keep the leftovers in an airtight food container in a fridge for up to 5 days. Just reheat them at 350°F for 2-3 minutes.
Per 1 Serving - Calories: 171, Carbohydrates: 8 g, Fat: 15 g, Protein: 3 g, Sugar: 5 g, Sodium: 307 mg.

KOREAN CAULIFLOWER BITES

Cooking Time: 1 Hours   **Yield:** 4 Servings

INGREDIENTS

- 1 head cauliflower
- 1 cup of all-purpose flour
- ½ cup +1 tablespoon of cornstarch
- 4 ½ tablespoons of Korean chili sauce
- 4 tablespoons of soy sauce
- 3 tablespoons of honey
- 1 tablespoon of garlic powder
- 2 ½ teaspoons of baking powder
- 1 teaspoon of sesame oil
- ½ teaspoon of minced garlic
- ½ teaspoon of grated ginger
- ½ teaspoon of rice vinegar

INSTRUCTIONS

1. Cut the cauliflower head into bite-sized florets. Mix 1 tablespoon of cornstarch with a pinch of baking powder, salt, and black pepper in a small bowl. Sprinkle this mixture over cauliflower florets to coat.
2. Whisk ½ cup of cornstarch, flour, garlic and baking powder in a large bowl. Add in 1 cup of cold water and stir to make batter.
3. Dip each cauliflower bite into the batter to coat evenly and shake off the excess. Put them on a wire rack to drip off any excess.
4. Spread oil inside the air fryer basket. Put the coated cauliflower inside the basket in a single layer. Air fry each batch at 350°F for 10-12 minutes until lightly golden brown. Repeat it to cook all the batches.
5. Cook the sauce. Whisk the soy sauce, Korean chili sauce, sesame oil, honey, vinegar, ginger, and garlic in a small saucepan. Bring it to a boil and remove from the heat. Pour it over the cooked cauliflower and stir to coat.
6. Serve and enjoy Korean Cauliflower Bites!

USEFUL NOTES

Per 1 Serving - Calories: 311, Carbohydrates: 69 g, Fat: 2 g, Protein: 8 g.

SPICED BEAN TACOS

Cooking Time: 20 Minutes **Yield:** 4 Servings

INGREDIENTS

- 4 corn tortillas
- 1 can of black beans
- 1 cup of yellow corn
- 1 diced avocado
- 1 diced Roma tomato
- 1 minced garlic clove
- 1 tablespoon of taco seasoning
- Parsley, for garnishing
- Lime wedges, for serving

INSTRUCTIONS

1. Preheat your air fryer to 400°F.
2. Spray some oil inside the silicone air fryer pot, add the minced garlic, and spray over with oil. Roast it at 400°F for 2-3 minutes.
3. Drain approximately half of the liquid from the can of beans. Add the can of black beans and 1 tablespoon of taco seasoning to the silicone pot. Stir it and spread the beans into a single layer.
4. Air fry everything at 380°F for 8 minutes, stirring halfway, until most of the juices are gone.
5. Make the tacos by layering the tortillas with black beans, corn, tomatoes, and avocados. Sprinkle over with the chopped parsley.
6. Serve with lime wedges. Enjoy your Spiced Bean Tacos!

USEFUL NOTES

You can store the cooked beans in an airtight food container in a fridge for up to 5 days. Just reheat them at 380°F for 3 minutes.
Per 1 Serving - Calories: 170, Carbohydrates: 21 g, Fat: 8 g, Protein: 7 g, Sugar: 1 g, Sodium: 56 mg.

CRISPY POTATO SKINS

Cooking Time: 40 Minutes **Yield:** 4 Servings

INGREDIENTS

- 3 russet potatoes
- 1 cup of shredded cheddar cheese
- 4 cooked bacon slices
- ½ cup of mayonnaise
- 1/3 cup of sour cream
- 2 tablespoons of chopped green onions
- 2 tablespoons of olive oil
- 1 ½ teaspoons of ranch dressing mix
- Ranch seasoning mix, to taste

INSTRUCTIONS

1. Wash and dry the potatoes. Put each potato inside the air fryer basket and spray some oil over them. Air fry them at 400°F for 35-45 minutes until soft. Spray generously with oil and cook at 400°F for 20 minutes.
2. Cool the potatoes completely and cut them in half. Scoop out the inside of the potato, leaving ¼" thick of the flesh along the sides and bottom of the potatoes.
3. Drizzle the inside of the potatoes with oil, season with salt, and ranch seasoning mix.
4. Put the cooked and crumbled bacon with shredded cheese on each potato.
5. Place the stuffed potatoes in the basket and fry them at 350°F for 6-10 minutes until cheese is melted.
6. Mix the sour cream, mayonnaise, and ranch dressing mix. Serve with the prepared dressing. Enjoy it!

USEFUL NOTES

You can store the cooked potatoes in an airtight food container in a fridge for up to 5 days. Just reheat them at 350°F for 3 minutes.

Per 1 Serving - Calories: 641, Carbohydrates: 34 g, Fat: 50 g, Protein: 14 g, Sugar: 2 g, Sodium: 953 mg.

EGGPLANT PARMESAN BITES

Cooking Time: 30 Minutes   **Yield:** 6 Servings

INGREDIENTS

- 1 large eggplant
- 2 cups of panko bread crumbs
- ½ cup of grated Parmesan cheese
- 2 eggs
- 1 tablespoon of Italian seasoning
- 2 teaspoons of garlic powder
- 1 ¼ teaspoon of sea salt
- 1 pinch of red pepper flakes

INSTRUCTIONS

1. Cut the eggplant into 1" slices. Sprinkle over ¼ teaspoon of sea salt to let them sweat.
2. Mix the Parmesan cheese, panko bread crumbs, garlic powder, Italian seasoning, red pepper flakes, and 1 teaspoon of salt on a shallow plate.
3. Whisk 2 eggs in a separate bowl.
4. Dip the eggplant slices into the whisked egg, then coat with the cheese-bread mixture.
5. Put the coated slices inside the air fryer basket and spray them with oil. Air fry them at 380°F for 12 minutes, stirring halfway through cooking.
6. Serve with any marinara sauce. Enjoy your Eggplant Parmesan Bites!

USEFUL NOTES

You can keep the leftovers in an airtight food container in a fridge for up to 5 days. Just reheat them at 380°F for 3 minutes.
Per 1 Serving- Calories: 157, Carbohydrates: 21 g, Fat: 5 g, Protein: 8 g, Sugar: 4 g, Sodium: 788 mg.

GARLIC MUSHROOMS

Cooking Time: 15 Minutes   **Yield:** 4 Servings

INGREDIENTS

- 1 pound of cleaned and sliced mushrooms
- 1 tablespoon of chopped parsley
- 1 tablespoon of garlic powder
- 2 teaspoons of soy sauce
- 1 tablespoon of olive oil
- Ground black pepper, to taste

INSTRUCTIONS

1. Preheat your air fryer to 400°F.
2. Mix the sliced mushrooms with soy sauce and olive oil. Season them with black pepper.
3. Put the prepared mushrooms inside the preheated basket, leaving some space between the slices.*
4. Air fry them at 400°F for 6-8 minutes, stirring halfway through cooking.
5. Remove them from the basket and mix with the garlic powder and parsley.
6. Serve warm and enjoy your Garlic Mushrooms!

USEFUL NOTES

* I recommend you cook in batches.
You can keep the leftovers in an airtight food container in a fridge for up to 3 days. Just reheat them at 400°F for 2 minutes.
Per 1 Serving - Calories: 42, Carbohydrates: 4 g, Fat: 4 g, Protein: 1 g, Sugar: 1 g, Sodium: 151 mg, Cholesterol: 0 mg.

ROASTED PARMESAN TOMATOES

Cooking Time: 10 Minutes   **Yield:** 2 Servings

INGREDIENTS

- 1-2 tomatoes
- Mozzarella cheese, to taste
- Salt and ground black pepper, to taste
- Fresh basil leaves, for garnishing
- Olive oil, to spray

INSTRUCTIONS

1. Cut tomatoes into thick slices and spread them in a single layer in a greased air fryer basket.
2. Season them with salt and black pepper and top with mozzarella cheese.
3. Roast them at 400°F for 3 minutes.
4. Serve with fresh basil on top. Enjoy your Roasted Parmesan Tomatoes!

USEFUL NOTES

* I recommend you cook in batches.
You can keep the leftovers in an airtight food container in a fridge for up to 5 days. Just reheat them at 350°F for 2 minutes.
Per 1 Serving - Calories: 159, Carbohydrates: 7 g, Fat: 10 g, Protein: 11 g, Sugar: 4 g, Sodium: 400 mg.

CABBAGE STEAK

Cooking Time: 20 Minutes   **Yield:** 4 Servings

INGREDIENTS

- 1 cabbage head
- 1 ½ teaspoons of Cajun seasoning
- 1 tablespoon of olive oil
- ½ teaspoon of salt
- ½ teaspoon of garlic powder

INSTRUCTIONS

1. Pour ¼ cup of water into the air fryer basket.* Preheat your air fryer to 350°F for 5 minutes. Spray some oil inside the basket.
2. Cut the cabbage head into the same thickness steaks (about ½").
3. Spread the olive oil over one side of each steak and sprinkle them with seasonings.
4. Put the cabbage steak oiled side down inside the preheated basket. Brush the top of the steak with olive oil and sprinkle over seasonings.
5. Air fry it at 360°F for 8-10 minutes till the cooked and get crispy.
6. Repeat the last 2 steps with the remaining steaks. Remember that the next steak will be done 1-2 minutes faster.
7. Serve warm and enjoy your Cabbage Steak!

USEFUL NOTES

* Adding some water inside the basket will help to make the cabbage softer. You can keep the leftovers in an airtight food container in a fridge for up to 2 days. Just reheat them at 360°F for 2-3 minutes.

Per 1 Serving - Calories: 97, Carbohydrates: 15 g, Fat: 4 g, Protein: 3 g, Sugar: 7 g, Sodium: 281 mg.

CRISPY POTATO WEDGES

Cooking Time: 35 Minutes   **Yield:** 4 Servings

INGREDIENTS

- 2 medium russet potatoes*
- 1 ½ tablespoons of olive oil
- ½ teaspoon of chili powder
- ½ teaspoon of parsley flakes
- ½ teaspoon of sea salt
- ½ teaspoon of ground paprika
- 1/8 teaspoon of ground black pepper

INSTRUCTIONS

1. Preheat your air fryer to 400°F.
2. Cut each potato in half lengthwise. Then, take each half and cut it in half lengthwise again. Finally, cut each resulting quarter in half lengthwise. You will get 16 wedges in total.
3. Put the potato wedges in a large bowl. Sprinkle them with paprika, chili, pepper, salt, parsley, and olive oil. Mix it to combine.
4. Transfer half of the potato wedges inside the preheated basket and air fry them at 400°F for 10 minutes. Flip them and cook for 5 minutes.
5. Repeat the last step with the remaining wedges.
6. Serve warm. Enjoy Crispy Potato Wedges!

USEFUL NOTES

* Use only a starchy potato variety, such as Yukon Golds or Russet potatoes. I recommend avoiding waxy potatoes, such as fingerlings, as they can fall apart while frying.

You can keep the leftovers in an airtight food container in a fridge for up to 5 days. Just reheat them at 400°F for 3 minutes.

Per 1 Serving - Calories: 129, Carbohydrates: 19 g, Fat: 5 g, Protein: 2 g, Sugar: 1 g, Sodium: 230 mg, Cholesterol: 0 mg.

SPICY FRENCH FRIES

Cooking Time: 30 Minutes **Yield:** 4 Servings

INGREDIENTS

- 2 medium russet potatoes*
- 1 ½ tablespoons of olive oil
- ½ teaspoon of herbs
- ½ teaspoon of chili powder
- ½ teaspoon of sea salt
- 1/8 teaspoon of ground black pepper

INSTRUCTIONS

1. Preheat your air fryer to 380°F.
2. Cut each potato into ¼" sticks. Drizzle them with olive oil and sprinkle with seasonings.
3. Put the potato sticks into the preheated basket in a single layer, leaving some space between pieces.
4. Air fry each batch at 380°F for 12-15 minutes, flipping halfway through cooking until crispy.
5. Once all potato sticks are cooked, put them back into the basket and air fry for 1-2 minutes to re-crisp.
6. Serve warm with your favorite sauce. Enjoy your Spicy French Fries!

USEFUL NOTES

* Use only a starchy potato variety, such as Yukon Golds or Russet potatoes. I recommend avoiding waxy potatoes, such as fingerlings, as they can fall apart while frying.

You can keep the leftovers in an airtight food container in a fridge for up to 5 days. Just reheat them at 380°F for 3-4 minutes.

Per 1 Serving - Calories: 120, Carbohydrates: 17 g, Fat: 5.4 g, Protein: 2 g, Sugar: 1 g, Sodium: 244 mg, Cholesterol: 0 mg.

ROASTED VEGETABLES

Cooking Time: 25 Minutes   **Yield:** 4 Servings

INGREDIENTS

- 2 cups of Brussels sprouts
- 10 cherry tomatoes
- 1 sliced red onion
- 1 chopped carrot
- 1 chopped bell pepper
- 1 tablespoon of olive oil
- 1 teaspoon of sea salt
- 1 teaspoon of garlic powder
- ½ teaspoon of ground black pepper
- ½ teaspoon of oregano
- ½ teaspoon of onion powder

INSTRUCTIONS

1. Preheat your air fryer to 375°F.
2. Put all the vegetables, seasonings, and olive oil in a large bowl and toss to combine.
3. Put some part of the vegetables inside the preheated basket and roast at 375°F for 10-15 minutes, shaking 1-2 times while cooking.
4. Repeat the last step with the remaining part of the vegetables.
5. Serve warm and enjoy your Roasted Vegetables!

USEFUL NOTES

If the vegetables come out too soggy, you overcrowd the air fryer basket or don't shake them while cooking.

Experiment with different combinations of vegetables. Add mushrooms, eggplant, or zucchini, or use seasonings like cumin and smoked paprika.

Per 1 Serving - Calories: 83, Carbohydrates: 11 g, Fat: 4 g, Protein: 3 g, Sugar: 5 g, Sodium: 596 mg.

CRISPY TOFU

Cooking Time: 50 Minutes   **Yield:** 3 Servings

INGREDIENTS

- 12 ounces of cubed extra firm tofu
- 1 tablespoon of cornstarch
- 1 tablespoon of soy sauce
- 1 teaspoon of garlic powder
- 1 teaspoon of olive oil
- ½ teaspoon of chili powder
- ½ teaspoon of ginger powder
- ¼ teaspoon of ground black pepper
- Sliced green onions, for garnishing

INSTRUCTIONS

1. Mix the tofu with oil, ginger powder, soy sauce, ground black pepper, chili powder, and garlic powder in a bowl. Add cornstarch to a bowl and toss to coat.
2. Preheat your air fryer to 400°F.
3. Place the coated tofu cubes into the hot basket in a single layer. Air fry them in batches at 400°F for 20 minutes, shaking every 5 minutes.
4. Serve warm with sliced green onions on the top. Enjoy your Crispy Tofu!

USEFUL NOTES

If you want to get crispy tofu, avoid overcrowding the basket. Otherwise, the tofu cubes will be steamed but not fried.

You can keep the leftovers in an airtight food container in a fridge for up to 5 days. Just reheat them at 400°F for 4-5 minutes.

Per 1 Serving - Calories: 95, Carbohydrates: 6 g, Fat: 4 g, Protein: 9 g, Sugar: 1 g, Sodium: 413 mg.

SWEET POTATO FRIES

Cooking Time: 20 Minutes   **Yield:** 2 Servings

INGREDIENTS

- 2 medium sweet potatoes
- 2 teaspoons of olive oil
- ¼ teaspoon of paprika
- ¼ teaspoon of garlic powder
- ½ teaspoon of salt
- 1/8 teaspoon of ground black pepper

INSTRUCTIONS

1. Preheat your air fryer to 380°F.
2. Peel each sweet potato and cut it into ¼" thick sticks.
3. Mix the potato sticks with olive oil, paprika, ground black pepper, salt, and garlic powder in a large bowl.
4. Spread some potato pieces inside the preheated basket. Cook it in 2-3 batches to avoid overcrowding. Air fry it at 380°F for 12 minutes, flipping halfway through cooking.
5. Serve warm with your favorite sauce. Enjoy your Sweet Potato Fries!

USEFUL NOTES

If you want to get crispy fries, avoid overcrowding the basket. Otherwise, the potato sticks will be steamed but not fried.

You can keep the leftovers in an airtight food container in a fridge for up to 4 days. Just reheat them at 360°F for 2 minutes.

Per 1 Serving - Calories: 149, Carbohydrates: 27 g, Fat: 4 g, Protein: 2 g, Sugar: 5 g, Sodium: 653 mg.

ROASTED BUTTERNUT SQUASH

Cooking Time: 1 Hour   **Yield:** 4 Servings

INGREDIENTS

- 1 small butternut squash
- 1 tablespoon of brown sugar
- 1 tablespoon of olive oil
- ¼ teaspoon of cinnamon
- Salt and ground black pepper, to taste

INSTRUCTIONS

1. Cut the butternut squash in half lengthwise.* Remove the seeds and pulp using a spoon.
2. Spread oil over the squash and sprinkle with cinnamon, brown sugar, salt, and black pepper.
3. Place the squash halves inside the air fryer basket, cut side up. Roast them at 350°F for 40-50 minutes until tender.
4. Serve warm** and enjoy your Roasted Butternut Squash!

USEFUL NOTES

* If your butternut squash is too large to fit your air fryer basket, cut it in quarters.
** It tastes good with a piece of butter on top.
You can keep the leftovers in an airtight food container in a fridge for up to 4 days. Just reheat them at 350°F for 3-5 minutes.
Per 1 Serving - Calories: 127, Carbohydrates: 25 g, Fat: 4 g, Protein: 2 g, Sugar: 7 g, Sodium: 8 mg.

GARLIC BROCCOLI

Cooking Time: 15 Minutes   **Yield:** 2 Servings

INGREDIENTS

- ½ pound of broccoli
- 1 tablespoon of grated Parmesan cheese
- 1 tablespoon of olive oil
- 1 minced garlic clove
- Salt and ground black pepper, to taste

INSTRUCTIONS

1. Preheat your air fryer to 400°F.
2. Wash and dry broccoli. Cut it into bite-sized pieces.
3. Mix the broccoli pieces, cheese, garlic, olive oil, salt, and ground black pepper in a large bowl. Toss to coat evenly.
4. Transfer the coated broccoli pieces into the preheated basket in a single layer.* Air fry them at 400°F for 5-7 minutes.
5. Serve warm and enjoy your Garlic Broccoli!

USEFUL NOTES

* I recommend cooking in batches to avoid overcrowding. Once all batches are cooked, put them back into the basket and air fry for 1-2 minutes to heat through.

You can keep the leftovers in an airtight food container in a fridge for up to 4 days. Just reheat them at 400°F for 2 minutes.

Per 1 Serving (1 Cup) - Calories: 112, Carbohydrates: 8 g, Fat: 8 g, Protein: 4 g, Sugar: 2 g, Sodium: 78 mg, Cholesterol: 2 mg.

ZUCCHINI FRITTERS

Cooking Time: 20 Minutes　　**Yield:** 4 Cakes

INGREDIENTS

- 2 medium zucchini
- 1/3 cup of grated Parmesan cheese
- 1/3 cup of flour
- 1 egg
- 1 sliced green onion
- 1 teaspoon of Italian seasoning
- 1 teaspoon of salt
- ½ teaspoon of garlic powder
- ½ teaspoon of baking powder
- Sour cream and chopped parsley, for serving

INSTRUCTIONS

1. Using a grater, shred the zucchini directly into a strainer placed over a towel. Once shredded, add salt to the zucchini and toss it. Allow the zucchini to sit for a while, as the salt will draw out the moisture.
2. Mix the flour, egg, cheese, garlic powder, baking powder, sliced green onion, and Italian seasoning in a large bowl.
3. Dry the shredded zucchini with a towel and add it to the bowl with the egg-flour mixture. Toss to combine.
4. Preheat your air fryer to 375ºF. Spray some oil inside the basket.
5. Form 4 cakes from the zucchini mixture* and put them into the preheated basket. Air fry them at 375ºF for 10 minutes, flip the cakes, and cook for 5 minutes more.
6. Serve warm with sour cream and chopped parsley. Enjoy your Zucchini Fritters!

USEFUL NOTES

* Flatten them more before serving if you want to get crispier fritters.
You can keep the leftovers in an airtight food container in a fridge for up to 3 days. Just reheat them at 375ºF for 2-3 minutes.
Per 1 Serving (1 Cake) - Calories: 110, Carbohydrates: 12 g, Fat: 4 g, Protein: 7 g, Sugar: 3 g, Sodium: 734 mg, Cholesterol: 48 mg.

FRIED SPAGHETTI SQUASH

Cooking Time: 40 Minutes   **Yield:** 4 Servings

INGREDIENTS

- 1 medium spaghetti squash
- ½ teaspoon of sea salt
- ¼ teaspoon of ground black pepper
- 1 tablespoon of olive oil

INSTRUCTIONS

1. Preheat your air fryer to 370°F.
2. Cut the spaghetti squash in half lengthwise.* Remove the seeds using a spoon.
3. Spread oil over the squash, and sprinkle with salt and black pepper.
4. Place the squash halves inside the air fryer basket, cut side up. Roast them at 370°F for 25-30 minutes until tender.
5. After cooking the squash, take a fork and gently run it along the strands of the squash. This action will help separate the strands, creating a spaghetti-like texture.
6. Serve warm* and enjoy your Fried Spaghetti Squash!

USEFUL NOTES

* It tastes good with a piece of butter on top.

You can keep the leftovers in an airtight food container in a fridge for up to 3 days. Just reheat them at 370°F for 3 minutes.

Per 1 Serving - Calories: 106, Carbohydrates: 17 g, Fat: 5 g, Protein: 2 g, Sugar: 7 g, Sodium: 332 mg.

CHEESE-BACON FRIES

Cooking Time: 40 Minutes   **Yield:** 6 Servings

INGREDIENTS

- 32 ounces (8 cups) of frozen french fries
- 1 ½ cups of cheddar cheese
- 3 tablespoons of cooked and crumbled bacon
- 2 sliced green onions
- 1 cup of brown gravy*
- ½ cup of sour cream*

INSTRUCTIONS

1. Preheat your air fryer to 390°F.
2. Place a small batch of frozen french fries inside the preheated basket. Air fry each batch at 390°F for 10-14 minutes until crispy.
3. Once all batches are cooked, put them back in the basket and reheat at 390°F for 2-3 minutes.
4. Sprinkle the cheese and bacon over the potatoes in the basket and air fry it at 390°F for 2-3 minutes.
5. Serve warm* and enjoy your Cheese-Bacon Fries!

USEFUL NOTES

* If using, drizzle with brown gravy and top with sour cream.
You can keep the leftovers in an airtight food container in a fridge for up to 3 days. Just reheat them at 390°F for 3-4 minutes.
Per 1 Serving - Calories: 577, Carbohydrates: 50 g, Fat: 37 g, Protein: 13 g, Sugar: 2 g, Sodium: 1257 mg, Cholesterol: 45 mg.

WONTON CHIPS

Cooking Time: 10 Minutes   **Yield:** 8 Servings

INGREDIENTS

- 16 wonton wrappers
- Olive oil
- Sea salt

INSTRUCTIONS

1. Preheat your air fryer to 350°F. Spray some oil inside the air fryer basket.
2. Cut the wonton wrappers diagonally, then cut each piece in half again. Put the cut wonton wrappers in the air fryer basket, leaving some space between them. Spray the wrappers with cooking oil to help them crisp up, and sprinkle a pinch of salt over them for added flavor.
3. Air fry each batch at 350°F for 3-5 minutes until crispy and lightly brown.
4. Serve and enjoy your Wonton Chips!

USEFUL NOTES

Cook chips in small batches so they will crisp up evenly.
I recommend adding seasonings immediately after cooking for better sticking.
Allow the chips to cool off completely before storing them to avoid moisture. You can keep the leftovers in an airtight food container or bag on the counter.
Per 1 Serving - Calories: 49, Carbohydrates: 9 g, Fat: 1 g, Protein: 1 g, Sodium: 232 mg, Cholesterol: 1 mg.

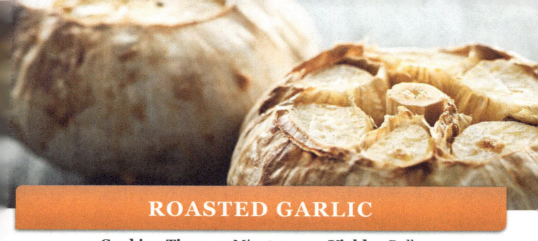

ROASTED GARLIC

Cooking Time: 35 Minutes   **Yield:** 3 Bulbs

INGREDIENTS

- 3 garlic bulbs
- 2 tablespoons of olive oil

INSTRUCTIONS

1. Preheat your air fryer to 380°F.
2. Cut off ¼ from the garlic tops to expose the cloves and drizzle with olive oil.
3. Wrap each garlic in foil and put it into the air fryer basket.
4. Fry them at 380°F for 30-35 minutes until lightly brown and very soft.
5. Remove the garlic from the basket and gently squeeze each clove to take it out.
6. Serve and enjoy your Roasted Garlic!

USEFUL NOTES

You can store the leftovers in the bulb in an airtight food container in a fridge for up to 1 week.
If you want to freeze the roasted garlic, squeeze the cloves from the skins and keep them in a ziplock bag for up to 4 months.
Per 1 Serving (1 Bulb) - Calories: 84, Carbohydrates: 1 g, Fat: 9 g, Protein: 1 g, Sodium: 1 mg.

POPCORN SHRIMP

Cooking Time: 30 Minutes   **Yield:** 4 Servings

INGREDIENTS

- 1 cup of panko bread crumbs
- 1 pound of uncooked peeled small shrimp
- ½ cup of all-purpose flour
- ½ cup of seasoned bread crumbs
- 2 eggs
- 2 tablespoons of water
- 2 teaspoons of garlic powder
- 1 teaspoon of smoked paprika
- ½ teaspoon of salt
- ½ teaspoon of ground black pepper

INSTRUCTIONS

1. Mix flour with salt and ground black pepper in a shallow bowl.
2. Whisk eggs with water in a separate bowl.
3. Stir the breadcrumbs, paprika, garlic powder, and black pepper & salt to taste in a third bowl.
4. Firstly, coat each shrimp with the flour, then dip it into the whisked egg, and finally, cover with the bread crumbs, gently pressing to adhere.
5. Preheat your air fryer to 400°F. Spray some oil over the coated shrimp. Transfer them into the preheated air fryer basket, leaving some space between pieces.
6. Fry each batch at 400°F for 2 minutes. Flip them and cook for an extra 2-3 minutes.
7. Serve and enjoy your Popcorn Shrimp!

USEFUL NOTES

You can keep the leftovers in an airtight food container in a fridge for up to 3 days.
Just reheat until crispy before serving.
Per 1 Serving - Calories: 292, Carbohydrates: 36 g, Fat: 5 g, Protein: 24 g, Sodium: 1276 mg, Cholesterol: 225 mg.

NACHOS

Cooking Time: 20 Minutes   **Yield:** 4 Servings

INGREDIENTS

- 2 cups of shredded cheese
- 2-3 cups of tortilla chips
- ½ cup of chopped tomatoes
- ¼ cup of black and green olives
- ¼ cup of yellow corn
- ¼ cup of chopped jalapenos *(optional)*
- 2 tablespoons of chopped cilantro *(optional)*

INSTRUCTIONS

1. Spread the tortilla chips in a single layer in the air fryer basket, ensuring they overlap slightly to eliminate any gaps between the chips.
2. Cover the chips with half of the cheese.
3. Put the next layer of chips. Top over with remaining cheese, olives, cilantro, and jalapenos.
4. Put the basket inside the air fryer and fry it at 320°F for 3-5 minutes until the cheese is melted.
5. Remove it from the basket and top with chopped tomatoes.
6. Serve with guacamole. Enjoy your Nachos!

USEFUL NOTES

Correctly overlapped chips prevent the cheese from dripping through the tray. The close arrangement of the chips helps create a stable base and ensures that the cheese and any other toppings stay on top of the chips during the cooking process.
Per 1 Serving - Calories: 527, Carbohydrates: 40 g, Fat: 34 g, Protein: 19 g, Sodium: 726 mg, Cholesterol: 59 mg.

PIZZA ROLLS

Cooking Time: 25 Minutes   **Yield:** 8 Rolls

INGREDIENTS

- 1 can of refrigerated pizza dough
- 1 ½ cups of shredded mozzarella cheese
- 1 cup of pizza sauce
- 2/3 cup of chopped pepperoni
- 1/3 cup of shredded Parmesan cheese
- ½ teaspoon of garlic powder

INSTRUCTIONS

1. Preheat your air fryer to 330°F.
2. Roll pizza dough out to about 12" x 8". Spoon half of the pizza sauce over the top of the dough.
3. Spread the cheese and pepperoni over the sauce. Roll the dough in a cinnamon roll style.
4. Cut it into 8 equal pieces. Pinch the bottom of each roll slightly to seal in the cheese.
5. Place them inside the preheated basket and bake at 330°F for 11-14 until the rolls are browned.
6. Serve with the remaining pizza sauce for dipping. Enjoy Pizza Rolls!

USEFUL NOTES

You can experiment with different toppings. If you plan to use toppings like mushrooms or pineapple, which tend to have a lot of moisture, cooking and squeezing them dry before adding to your dish is recommended. It helps prevent excess moisture from making the crust soggy.

You can freeze these cooled pizza rolls in a zippered bag and keep them in a freezer for up to 2 months. Just reheat them at 350°F for 15 minutes.

Per 1 Serving (1 Roll) - Calories: 254, Carbohydrates: 26 g, Fat: 11 g, Protein: 12 g, Sodium: 878 mg, Cholesterol: 29 mg.

FRIED CALAMARI

Cooking Time: 35 Minutes   **Yield:** 4 Servings

INGREDIENTS

- 1 ½ pounds of squid rings
- 3 eggs
- 1 cup of flour
- 1 cup of cornmeal
- 1 cup of panko breadcrumbs
- 2 teaspoons of Old Bay spice
- 1 teaspoon of ground black pepper
- 1 teaspoon of salt

INSTRUCTIONS

1. Preheat your air fryer to 375°F.
2. Mix the flour, black pepper, and salt in a large bowl.
3. Whisk the eggs in a separate bowl.
4. Combine the cornmeal, breadcrumbs, and Old Bay spice in a third bowl.
5. Firstly, cover each squid ring with flour, dip it into the whisked eggs, and then coat it with the cornmeal-breadcrumbs mixture.
6. Put the coated rings in a single layer inside the preheated basket. Air fry each batch at 375°F for 15 minutes, flipping halfway through cooking. Avoid overcooking that can lead to tough and rubbery.
7. Serve warm with marinara sauce and lime wedges. Enjoy Fried Calamari!

USEFUL NOTES

You can keep the leftovers in an airtight food container in a fridge for up to 3 days. Just reheat at 350°F for 8 minutes before serving.
I don't recommend freezing the leftovers.
Per 1 Serving - Calories: 530, Carbohydrates: 69 g, Fat: 8 g, Protein: 39 g, Sodium: 669 mg, Cholesterol: 519 mg.

STUFFED MUSHROOMS

Cooking Time: 35 Minutes   **Yield:** 16 Mushrooms

INGREDIENTS

- 16 medium mushrooms
- 1/3 cup of shredded cheddar cheese
- 8 ounces of cream cheese
- 3 crumbled bacon slices
- 2 tablespoons of grated Parmesan cheese
- 1 sliced green onion
- ¼ teaspoon of salt
- ¼ teaspoon of garlic powder
- 1/8 teaspoon of smoked paprika

INSTRUCTIONS

1. Preheat your air fryer to 350°F.
2. Rinse and dry mushrooms. Cut out the stems from the caps and chop them.
3. Mix the chopped mushroom stems, softened cream cheese, bacon, Parmesan cheese, green onion, seasonings, and 3 tablespoons of cheddar cheese.
4. Spoon each mushroom cap with the prepared mixture. Place the stuffed caps inside the preheated basket and fry them at 350°F for 6 minutes.
5. Open the basket and spread the remaining cheddar cheese over the mushroom tops. Cook for an extra 2 minutes.
6. Remove them from the basket and cook another batch. Let it cool for 5 minutes before serving. Serve warm and enjoy it!

USEFUL NOTES

Sometimes the mushroom caps can fall sideways while opening or closing the basket. In this case, you should put a piece of foil inside and fold the sides to hold them upright.

You can keep the leftovers in an airtight food container in a fridge for up to 3 days. Just reheat at 400°F for 4-5 minutes before serving.

Per 1 Serving - Calories: 73, Carbohydrates: 1 g, Fat: 7 g, Protein: 2 g, Sodium: 120 mg, Cholesterol: 20 mg.

PIZZA BAGELS

Cooking Time: 10 Minutes   **Yield:** 2 Servings

INGREDIENTS

- 2 mini bagels
- 1 cup of mozzarella cheese
- ½ cup of pizza sauce
- Pepperoni slices

INSTRUCTIONS

1. Preheat your air fryer to 400°F.
2. Cut the bagels in half crosswise. Spoon each bagel with sauce and cheese and top with pepperoni slices.
3. Transfer the bagels to the preheated basket and fry them at 400°F for 5 minutes until the cheese is totally melted and slightly browned.
4. Serve warm and enjoy Pizza Bagels!

USEFUL NOTES

If you like to eat extra-crispy pizzas, cook them a little longer until the bottoms get extra crunchy.

You can experiment with different toppings, like mushrooms, sausage, olives, ham, pineapple, tomatoes, chicken, or bacon.

Per 1 Serving - Calories: 298, Carbohydrates: 27 g, Fat: 13 g, Protein: 18 g, Sodium: 896 mg.

FRIED CHEESE STICKS

Cooking Time: 2 Hours   **Yield:** 24 Sticks

INGREDIENTS

- 12 mozzarella cheese strings, cut in half
- 1 large beaten egg
- ½ cup of plain bread crumbs
- ½ cup of all-purpose flour
- ½ cup of ranch dressing, for serving
- ½ cup of marinara sauce, for serving
- 1 ½ teaspoons of Italian seasoning
- ¼ pinch of salt
- Ground black pepper, to taste

INSTRUCTIONS

1. Cut each mozzarella stick in half, spread them on a parchment-lined baking sheet, and flash freeze for 20 minutes.
2. Once they are frozen, cover each stick with the flour and dip into the egg. I recommend doing it with a fork.
3. After flash-freezing the mozzarella halves, roll them in the seasoned breadcrumbs until thoroughly coated. Place the coated cheese sticks back onto the baking sheet and freeze for 45 minutes or more.
4. Spray oil inside the basket and preheat it to 400°F. Spray the first batch of mozzarella sticks with some oil and place them inside the basket. Air fry at 400°F for 4-6 minutes until crispy and golden.
5. Cook another batch. Be sure to spray some oil before cooking.
6. Serve warm with ranch dressing and marinara sauce. Enjoy it!

USEFUL NOTES

You can keep the leftovers in an airtight food container in a fridge for up to 3 days. Just reheat at 400°F for 2 minutes before serving.
Per 1 Serving (1 Cheese Sticks) - Calories: 87, Carbohydrates: 5 g, Fat: 6 g, Protein: 4 g, Sodium: 211 mg, Cholesterol: 16 mg.

BANANA CHIPS

Cooking Time: 20 Minutes   **Yield:** 6 Servings

INGREDIENTS

- 3 large plantains or raw bananas
- 3 tablespoons of coconut oil
- 3 teaspoons of turmeric powder
- 2 teaspoons of salt

INSTRUCTIONS

1. Preheat your air fryer to 350°F.
2. Cut off the ends of green bananas using a knife and peel them.
3. Mix salt and 2 teaspoons of turmeric in a water bowl and soak the peeled bananas for 5-10 minutes.
4. Dry the soaked bananas and slice them on a mandolin. Coat them with coconut oil and the remaining turmeric.
5. Place the first part of the banana slices inside the preheated basket and fry at 350°F for 10 minutes. If needed, add extra 5 minutes.
6. Repeat the last step with the remaining banana slices.
7. Serve* and enjoy Banana Chips!

USEFUL NOTES

* Sprinkle some salt, curry powder, garlic powder, or lime juice over the cooked slices if you like.
You can keep the leftovers in an airtight food container for up to 3 weeks at room temperature.
Per 1 Serving - Calories: 220, Carbohydrates: 76 g, Fat: 8 g, Protein: 4 g, Sodium: 267 mg, Cholesterol: 0 mg.

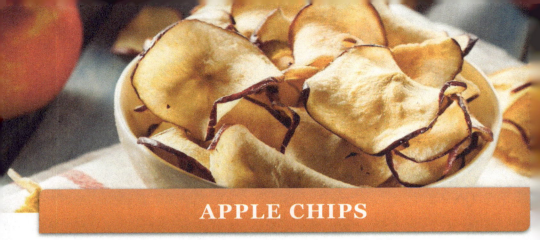

APPLE CHIPS

Cooking Time: 15 Minutes   **Yield:** 3 Cups

INGREDIENTS

- 3 large apples*
- ¾ teaspoon of ground cinnamon
- Pinch of salt

INSTRUCTIONS

1. Preheat your air fryer to 390°F.
2. Wash the apples thoroughly and core them. Make 1/8" thick slices using a sharp knife or mandolin.
3. Add salt and cinnamon to the apple slices. Mix to cover the pieces.
4. Put the apple slices on a single layer without them overlapping. Air fry them at 390°F for 8 minutes, flipping halfway through cooking. If you want to eat crispier chips, add for 1 minute at a time and check the crisp level.
5. Serve* and enjoy Apple Chips!

USEFUL NOTES

* I recommend using crisp and sweet apples, like Fuji, Pink Lady, Jazz, or Honeycrisp.

You can keep the leftovers in an airtight food container for up to 6 days at room temperature.

Per 1 Serving (1 Cup) - Calories: 65, Carbohydrates: 18 g, Fat: 0 g, Protein: 0 g, Sodium: 4 mg, Cholesterol: 0 mg.

BACON-WRAPPED DATES

Cooking Time: 30 Minutes   **Yield:** 12 Dates

INGREDIENTS

- 12 large Medjool dates
- ¼ cup of soft blue cheese or goat cheese
- 6 bacon strips

INSTRUCTIONS

1. Using a sharp knife, carefully make a lengthwise slit on one side of each date. Gently remove the pit from each date.
2. Add 1 teaspoon of cheese inside each date.*
3. Cut each bacon strip in half widthwise to get 12 pieces.
4. Place the stuffed date on one end of the bacon slice. Roll it up and fix it with a toothpick.
5. Preheat your air fryer to 390°F.
6. Put the wrapped and stuffed dates inside the preheated basket, try to avoid touching each other. Air fry at 390°F for 8 minutes, then shake the basket to flip the dates over. Cook for 3-5 minutes more until crispy bacon.
7. Serve and enjoy Bacon-Wrapped Dates!

USEFUL NOTES

* Don't overfill the dates; the cheese will leak out from them.
You can keep the leftovers in an airtight food container in a fridge for up to 3 days.
Per 1 Serving (1 Date) - Calories: 84, Carbohydrates: 18 g, Fat: 2 g, Protein: 1 g, Sodium: 19 mg, Cholesterol: 3 mg.

BANANAS

Cooking Time: 15 Minutes   **Yield:** 4 Servings

INGREDIENTS

- 2 large bananas
- 2 tablespoons of melted coconut oil
- 1 tablespoon of brown sugar
- 1 teaspoon of cinnamon
- ¼ teaspoon of nutmeg
- 1/8 teaspoon of cloves

INSTRUCTIONS

1. Cut lengthwise each banana in half and put them on a plate.
2. Mix the sugar with all spices in a small bowl.
3. Using a brush, apply melted coconut oil onto the cut side of the bananas. Then sprinkle the sugar mixture generously over the bananas, ensuring they are fully coated with the mixture.
4. Spray some oil inside the air fryer basket and put in the bananas.
5. Air fry them at 400°F for 8-10 minutes until caramelized and golden brown.
6. Serve warm with a scoop of vanilla ice cream and cinnamon. Enjoy your Bananas!

USEFUL NOTES

You can keep the leftovers in an airtight food container in a fridge for up to 3 days. Just reheat before serving.

Per 1 Serving - Calories: 134, Carbohydrates: 19 g, Fat: 7 g, Protein: 1 g, Sugar: 11 g, Sodium: 2 mg, Cholesterol: 0 mg.

APPLE GALETTE

Cooking Time: 35 Minutes   **Yield:** 6 Servings

INGREDIENTS

- 2-3 medium tart apples
- 1 store-bought pie crust
- 4 tablespoons of brown sugar
- 2 tablespoons of lemon juice
- 1 teaspoon of ground cinnamon

INSTRUCTIONS

1. Peel and core the apples. Cut them into thin slices. Combine the apples with cinnamon, lemon juice, and 3 tablespoons of brown sugar.
2. Lay parchment paper on a flat surface and transfer the dough onto it. Arrange the apples in the dough's center, leaving a border of about 1" around the edges.
3. Gently fold one edge towards the center, covering a portion of the filling. Continue folding all the way around the crust. Sprinkle over with the remaining sugar.
4. Cut the parchment paper excess around the galette to fit your air fryer. Transfer it to your basket.
5. Bake it at 360°F for 16-30 minutes until the apples are soft, the dough is lightly brown. Let it cool for 20 minutes before slicing. Serve and enjoy it!

USEFUL NOTES

Check the size of your basket to be sure what exact size will fit. The actual size of the galette should be 1" to 1 ½" smaller in diameter.
You can keep the leftovers at room temperature for up to 2 days.
Per 1 Serving - Calories: 209, Carbohydrates: 35 g, Fat: 8 g, Protein: 2 g, Sugar: 18 g, Sodium: 123 mg.

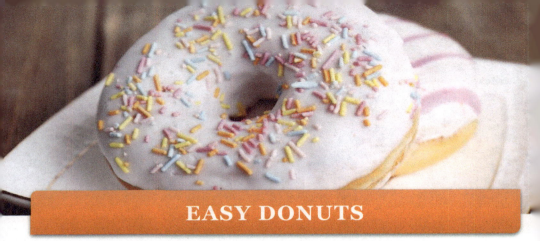

EASY DONUTS

Cooking Time: 30 Minutes   **Yield:** 8 Servings

INGREDIENTS

- 1 ¾ cups of self-rising flour
- 1 ½ cups of powdered sugar
- 1 cup of vanilla yogurt
- 2 tablespoons of rainbow sprinkles
- 1-2 tablespoons of water

INSTRUCTIONS

1. Mix flour with yogurt in a bowl until a thick consistency. If it's too thin, add more flour; if it's too thick, add more yogurt.
2. Flour your working surface. Put the dough and knead it several times until it becomes elastic. Divide the dough into 8 equal portions and roll them out into a long, sausage-like shape. Connect ends to form a circular shape resembling a donut. Repeat it with the remaining dough.
3. Line your air fryer basket with parchment paper. Put in 2-4 donuts, leaving ½ inch apart. Fry them at 400°F for 7-8 minutes until firm outside. Cook other batches.
4. Meantime, add sugar and water to a large bowl. Mix it well until smooth and thick.
5. Dip each cooked donut into the prepared glaze and place them on a wire rack. Sprinkle over with rainbow jimmies.
6. Serve and enjoy your Easy Donuts!

USEFUL NOTES

Keep the leftovers in an airtight food container in a fridge for up to 5 days. If you want to freeze, put the cooked donuts in an airtight food container and keep them in a freezer for up to 6 months.
Per 1 Serving - Calories: 125, Carbohydrates: 19 g, Fat: 2 g, Protein: 5 g.

QUICK SCONES

Cooking Time: 40 Minutes   **Yield:** 8 Servings

INGREDIENTS

- 2 cups of self-rising flour
- ¼ cup of sugar
- ¼ cup of unsalted butter*
- 1/3 cup of buttermilk
- 1 large egg
- 2 tablespoons of milk
- 1 tablespoon of Demerara sugar (optional)
- 1 teaspoon of baking powder

INSTRUCTIONS

1. Mix the flour with baking powder in a bowl. Add in the cubed butter and rub it with fingertips until it resembles fine breadcrumbs. Mix in the sugar.
2. Combine the buttermilk and egg. Gradually pour this mixture into the mixing bowl, stirring until a soft, sticky dough forms.
3. Transfer the dough onto your floured work surface, pat it down to form a square 1-2 cm in height. Ensure that the square is shorter than a 6 cm fluted cutter. To cut out the scones, press the cutter straight into the dough without twisting it, then lift it straight out. Repeat it with all dough. Brush the top of the scones with milk and sprinkle with Demerara sugar.
4. Preheat your air fryer to 350°F. Line the basket with parchment paper and place the scones on it. Bake them at 350°F for 15 minutes until golden and well-risen.
5. Serve with clotted cream and jam on top.

USEFUL NOTES

Per 1 Serving (1 Scone) - Calories: 219, Carbohydrates: 33 g, Fat: 7 g, Protein: 5 g, Sugar: 9 g, Sodium: 69 mg, Cholesterol: 38 mg.

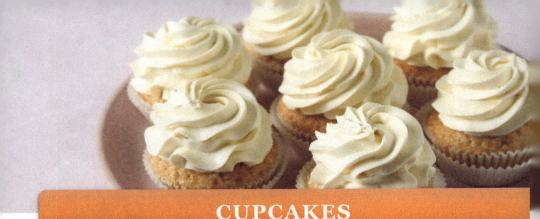

CUPCAKES

Cooking Time: 35 Minutes   **Yield:** 8 Servings

INGREDIENTS

- 2 cups of self-rising flour
- 2 cups of powdered sugar
- 1 ¼ cups of superfine sugar
- ½ cup of margarine
- ½ cup of unsalted butter
- ½ cup of milk
- 1/3 cup of heavy cream
- 2 large eggs
- 2 teaspoons of vanilla extract
- 1 teaspoon of vanilla bean paste

INSTRUCTIONS

1. Mix the flour, superfine sugar, margarine, eggs, milk, and vanilla extract in a mixing bowl. Using an electric hand mixer, beat it until the batter is smooth in texture.
2. Divide it between 8 large paper cup cases and put into the air fryer.
3. Bake them at 325°F for 23-25 minutes until golden and risen. Check the doneness by inserting a toothpick in the middle of them; it should come out clean.
4. Add the powdered sugar, butter, heavy cream, and vanilla bean paste to a bowl. Start whisking at a low-speed setting to combine the ingredients. Increase the speed to medium-high and continue beating until the frosting is consistent with peaks. Transfer it into a piping bag fitted with a large star tip.
5. Pipe a generous swirl of frosting over the cupcakes. Start from the center and work outward in a spiral motion to create an attractive design. Serve and enjoy it!

USEFUL NOTES

Per 1 Serving (1 Cup) - Calories: 366, Carbohydrates: 56 g, Fat: 14 g, Protein: 5 g, Sugar: 32 g, Sodium: 159 mg, Cholesterol: 43 mg.

APPLE FRITTERS

Cooking Time: 20 Minutes   **Yield:** 12-14 Servings

INGREDIENTS

- 2 cups of all-purpose flour
- 2 cups of powdered sugar
- 1 cup of apple cider or apple juice
- ½ cup of granulated sugar
- 2 large apples
- 2 eggs
- 3 tablespoons of melted butter
- 1 tablespoon of baking powder
- 1 ½ teaspoons of cinnamon
- 1 teaspoon of salt
- 1 teaspoon vanilla
- ½ + ¼ teaspoon of ground nutmeg
- ¼ teaspoon of ground cloves

INSTRUCTIONS

1. Peel, core, and chop the apples into ¼" pieces. Spread them on a kitchen towel to pat the moisture off.
2. Mix the flour, baking powder, granulated sugar, salt, ground cloves, 1 teaspoon of cinnamon, and ½ teaspoon of cinnamon in a bowl. Add in the apples and stir them.
3. Whisk the eggs, vanilla, butter, and ¾ cup of apple cider in a small bowl. Pour it into the flour mixture and stir to combine.
4. Preheat your air fryer to 390°F. Line the basket with parchment paper. Take 3-4 spoons of the dough to make a fritter and put it inside the basket. Repeat it with the remaining dough. Spray the tops with oil.
5. Air fry them at 390°F for 6 minutes, flip and continue cooking for 4 minutes more.
6. Meantime, mix the powdered sugar, ¼ cup of apple cider, ½ teaspoon of cinnamon, and ¼ teaspoon of nutmeg until smooth. Drizzle it over the baked fritters. Coll for 10 minutes after coating with the glaze. Serve and enjoy it!

USEFUL NOTES

Per 1 Serving - Calories: 221, Carbohydrates: 46 g, Fat: 3 g, Protein: 3 g.

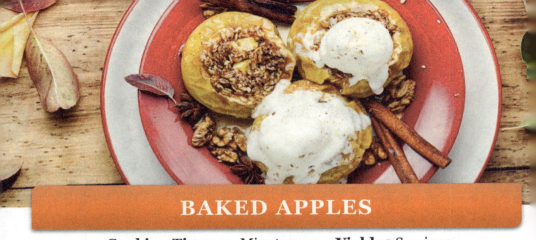

BAKED APPLES

Cooking Time: 20 Minutes　　**Yield:** 2 Servings

INGREDIENTS

- 2 apples
- 1/3 cup of old-fashioned oats
- 1 tablespoon + 1 teaspoon of melted butter
- 1 tablespoon of maple syrup
- 1 teaspoon of all-purpose flour
- 1 teaspoon of cinnamon

INSTRUCTIONS

1. Cut apples halfway through the stem, and remove the stem, core, and seeds. Brush the cut side with 1 teaspoon of butter and sprinkle ½ teaspoon of cinnamon over this side.
2. Combine the old-fashioned oats, maple syrup, flour, 1 tablespoon of butter, and ½ teaspoon of cinnamon in a small bowl. Spoon the prepared mixture on top of the apple halves.
3. Transfer the stuffed apple halves to your air fryer basket. Bake them at 350°F for 15 minutes until softened.
4. Serve warm with cream or ice cream on top. Enjoy your Baked Apples!

USEFUL NOTES

I recommend using Pink Lady apples, but Honeycrisp, Golden Delicious, or Granny Smith would also work well.

You can keep the leftovers in an airtight food container for up to 2 days at room temperature.

Per 1 Serving- Calories: 247, Carbohydrates: 43 g, Fat: 9 g, Protein: 3 g, Sugar: 25 g, Sodium: 65 mg, Cholesterol: 20 mg.

BREAD PUDDING

Cooking Time: 25 Minutes   **Yield:** 6 Servings

INGREDIENTS

- 2 cups of cubed bread
- 2/3 cup of heavy cream
- ¼ cup of chocolate chips
- ¼ cup of sugar
- 1 egg
- ½ teaspoon of vanilla extract

INSTRUCTIONS

1. Spray some oil inside the baking dish that can fit your air fryer.
2. Spread the bread cubes in the baking dish and sprinkle the chocolate chips.
3. Whisk the egg, sugar, vanilla, and whipped cream separately. Pour it over the bread cubes and let it stand for 5 minutes.
4. Put the baking dish inside the basket and bake it at 350°F for 15 minutes until cooked through.
5. Serve and enjoy your Bread Pudding!

USEFUL NOTES

Use day-old bread for this recipe. If you can plan ahead, slice the bread into cubes and allow it to dry overnight.

You can keep the leftovers in an airtight food container in a fridge for up to 4 days. It is recommended to reheat it in the air fryer for a few minutes before serving.

Per 1 Serving - Calories: 375, Carbohydrates: 53 g, Fat: 14 g, Protein: 9 g, Sugar: 18 g, Sodium: 425 mg, Cholesterol: 37 mg.

NUTELLA COOKIES

Cooking Time: 15 Minutes   **Yield:** 32 Servings

INGREDIENTS

- 1 ¼ cups of Nutella
- 1 cup of all-purpose flour
- 2 large eggs

INSTRUCTIONS

1. Combine the Nutella, flour, and eggs in a mixing bowl.
2. Line your air fryer basket with parchment paper. Scoop the prepared butter onto the parchment paper, leaving some space between each cookie.
3. Bake it at 340°F for 4 minutes until cooked through.
4. Serve and enjoy your Nutella Cookies!

USEFUL NOTES

It is recommended to bake cookies in batches. Don't overcrowd the basket. You can store the leftovers in an airtight food container at room temperature for up to 3 days.
Per 1 Serving (1 Cookie) - Calories: 82, Carbohydrates: 10 g, Fat: 4 g, Protein: 1 g, Sugar: 6 g, Sodium: 9 mg, Cholesterol: 12 mg.

CARAMELIZED PEACHES

Cooking Time: 15 Minutes   **Yield:** 4 Servings

INGREDIENTS

- 4 peaches*
- 3 tablespoons of brown sugar
- 3 tablespoons of butter
- 2 teaspoons of olive oil
- 1 teaspoon of ground cinnamon

INSTRUCTIONS

1. Preheat your air fryer to 350°F.
2. Mix the butter, sugar, and cinnamon in a small bowl.
3. Wash, dry, and cut the peaches* in half, removing the pits. Drizzle the cut side of the peaches with olive oil.
4. Put the peach halves inside the preheated basket and air fry them at 350°F for 5 minutes.
5. Take a spoonful of the butter mixture and add it to the peaches. Continue cooking for 5-6 minutes more until the fruits are caramelized on top.
6. Serve with granola, nuts, and ice cream on top. Enjoy your Caramelized Peaches!

USEFUL NOTES

* I strongly recommend cooking only from fresh peaches instead of canned or frozen.

You can keep the leftovers in an airtight food container in a fridge for up to 3 days. Just reheat at 350°F for 1-2 minutes before serving.

Per 1 Serving (2 Peach Halves) - Calories: 208, Carbohydrates: 21 g, Fat: 14 g, Protein: 2 g, Sugar: 21 g, Sodium: 4 mg, Cholesterol: 31 mg.

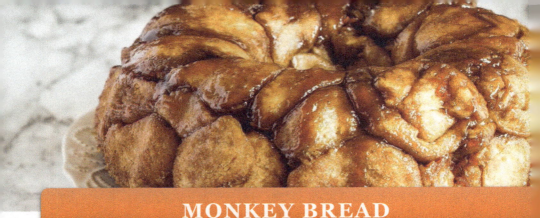

MONKEY BREAD

Cooking Time: 1 Hour   **Yield:** 6 Servings

INGREDIENTS

- 12 pre-made frozen dinner rolls (thawed to room temperature)
- ½ cup of powdered sugar
- ½ cup of brown sugar
- 4 tablespoons of melted butter
- 1-2 tablespoons of milk
- 1 teaspoon of cinnamon
- ½ teaspoon of vanilla

INSTRUCTIONS

1. Combine the cinnamon with brown sugar in a small bowl. Add 2 tablespoons of melted butter in a separate bowl.
2. Take an oven-safe pan that fits your air fryer and spread 2 tablespoons of butter inside it.
3. Cut the thawed rolls in half, roll each piece in the melted butter, dip into the sugar-cinnamon mixture, and transfer inside the pan. Repeat it with all rolls.
4. Once all rolls are inside the basket, pour the remaining butter and sprinkle with sugar. Leave it for 30 minutes to let the rolls rise. Cover the top of the rolls with foil to prevent them from burning. Bake it at 340°F for 14-18 minutes until fully cooked. Remove the foil and bake for 1-3 minutes more.
5. Make a glaze. Whisk the milk, powdered sugar, and vanilla. Serve on a plate with the prepared glaze on top. Enjoy it!

USEFUL NOTES

It's a great option for a Christmas breakfast.
Per 1 Serving - Calories: 402, Carbohydrates: 75 g, Fat: 5 g, Protein: 9 g, Sugar: 5 g, Sodium: 708 mg.

CARROT CAKE

Cooking Time: 40 Minutes   **Yield:** 8 Servings

INGREDIENTS

- 1 ½ cups of peeled and grated carrot
- 1 cup of all-purpose flour
- ½ cup of brown sugar
- ½ cup of sugar
- ½ cup of olive oil
- ½ cup of chopped walnuts
- ¼ cup of orange juice
- 2 large eggs
- 1 teaspoon of vanilla
- 1 teaspoon of ground cinnamon
- 1 teaspoon of baking soda
- ½ teaspoon of ground nutmeg

INSTRUCTIONS

1. Mix the flour, nutmeg, cinnamon, and baking soda in a medium bowl.
2. Whisk the eggs, sugar, brown sugar, and vanilla extract in a large bowl. Pour in oil with orange juice and mix. Once combined, add in the flour mixture and mix well until a smooth batter.
3. Stir in the shredded carrot and chopped walnuts until well combined.
4. Line 8" round cake pan with parchment paper. Lightly spray the inside of the pan with oil. Pour in the prepared batter, spreading evenly.
5. Put the cake pan inside the air fryer and bake it at 320°F for 20 minutes. Cover the top with foil and bake for 10 minutes until a toothpick comes out clean after inserting it in the cake center.
6. Serve and enjoy your Carrot Cake!

USEFUL NOTES

You can keep the leftovers in an airtight food container for up to 2 days at room temperature.

Per 1 Serving - Calories: 191, Carbohydrates: 41 g, Fat: 1 g, Protein: 3 g, Sugar: 28 g, Sodium: 176 mg, Cholesterol: 47 mg.

BANANA CAKE

Cooking Time: 40 Minutes   **Yield:** 4 Servings

INGREDIENTS

- 1 cup of self-rising flour
- 1/3 cup of brown sugar
- 1 mashed banana
- 1 egg
- 3 ½ tablespoons of butter
- 2 tablespoons of honey
- ½ teaspoon of ground cinnamon
- Pinch of salt

INSTRUCTIONS

1. Preheat your air fryer to 350°F. Spray some oil inside an 8" round cake pan.
2. Whisk the butter and sugar in a bowl using an electric mixer until you reach a creamy consistency.
3. Mix the egg, mashed banana, and honey in a separate bowl. Combine it with the butter mixture until smooth.
4. Add the cinnamon, flour, and salt to the butter-banana mixture. Mix it well to make a smooth batter. Transfer it to an oiled pan.
5. Put the prepared pan in the air fryer and bake at 350°F for 30 minutes. You can check the doneness by inserting a toothpick inside the cake center; it should come out clean.
6. Serve and enjoy your Banana Cake!

USEFUL NOTES

You can keep the leftovers in an airtight food container for up to 2 days at room temperature.
You can also freeze the cooked cake in a fridge for up to 6 months.
Per 1 Serving - Calories: 347, Carbohydrates: 57 g, Fat: 12 g, Protein: 5 g, Sugar: 30 g, Sodium: 531 mg, Cholesterol: 73 mg.

BLUEBERRY CRISP

Cooking Time: 25 Minutes **Yield:** 2 Servings

INGREDIENTS

- 1 cup of frozen blueberries*
- 3 tablespoons of quick-cooking oats
- 1 ½ tablespoons + 2 teaspoons of all-purpose flour
- 1 ½ tablespoons of softened salted butter
- 1 ½ tablespoons of brown sugar
- 1 teaspoon of lemon juice
- ½ teaspoon of ground cinnamon
- Pinch of salt

INSTRUCTIONS

1. Preheat your air fryer to 360°F.
2. Mix the blueberries, lemon juice, salt, and 2 teaspoons of all-purpose flour in a small bowl. Divide the prepared mixture between two 1-cup ramekins.
3. Combine the oats, cinnamon, brown sugar, and 1 ½ tablespoons of all-purpose flour in a small bowl. Add in the softened butter and stir until a crumbly mixture. Sprinkle over the blueberries.
4. Put the ramekins inside the air fryer and bake at 360°F for 12-14 minutes until golden-brown top.
5. Serve warm and enjoy your Blueberry Crisp!

USEFUL NOTES

* Experiment with any other fruits you like.
** Serve with a scoop of vanilla ice cream. Perfect combination.
You can keep the leftovers in an airtight food container for up to 3 days at room temperature.
Per 1 Serving - Calories: 217, Carbohydrates: 32 g, Fat: 10 g, Protein: 2 g, Sugar: 17 g, Sodium: 143 mg, Cholesterol: 23 mg.

BROWNIES

Cooking Time: 20 Minutes   **Yield:** 4 Servings

INGREDIENTS

- ¾ cup of sugar
- ½ cup of all-purpose flour
- ¼ cup of melted unsalted butter
- 6 tablespoons of unsweetened cocoa powder
- 2 large eggs
- 1 tablespoon of olive oil
- ½ teaspoon of vanilla extract
- ¼ teaspoon of baking powder
- ¼ teaspoon of salt

INSTRUCTIONS

1. Preheat your air fryer to 330°F. Grease your 7" baking pan with some oil.
2. Combine the cocoa powder, flour, butter, sugar, eggs, oil, baking powder, salt, and vanilla extract in a large bowl until well combined.
3. Transfer the prepared batter to the greased baking pan and smooth out the top.
4. Put the baking pan inside the preheated air fryer. Bake it at 330°F for 15 minutes. You can check the doneness by inserting a toothpick inside the cake center; it should come out clean.
5. Let it cool for 10-15 minutes before cutting.
6. Serve and enjoy your Brownies!

USEFUL NOTES

You can add any favorite nuts before baking the brownies. The amount is about ¼ cup.

You can store the leftovers in an airtight food container at room temperature for up to 3 days.

Per 1 Serving - Calories: 385, Carbohydrates: 54 g, Fat: 18 g, Protein: 6 g, Sugar: 38 g, Sodium: 181 mg, Cholesterol: 112 mg.

CONCLUSION

Congratulations! You have now completed my new book.

With the knowledge of simple, quick, and, most importantly, delicious recipes for your air fryer, you are now equipped to surprise yourself, your family, and your friends with an array of new and delightful dishes, snacks, and even desserts.

By embracing these recipes, not only will you savor mouthwatering meals, but you will also contribute to your well-being and enhance overall health by reducing the consumption of oil. It's truly remarkable!

Now, there's just one task left for you: Select a recipe and let the magic unfold in your kitchen! I would be thrilled to witness the fruits of your culinary adventures through the reviews for my book!

Take good care of yourself and enjoy a long, joyful life filled with delicious food and happiness!

LEAVE YOUR REVIEW

As an independent author with a small marketing budget, reviews are my livelihood on this platform. If you enjoyed this book, I'd appreciate it if you could leave your honest feedback on Amazon. You can do it by scanning the QR code below.

I read EVERY single review because I love the feedback from MY readers!

Thank you for staying with me!

It's so important to see your feedback!

RECIPE INDEX

Almonds
Almond Crusted Chicken, 31

Apples
Apple Chips, 96
Apple Fritters. 103
Apple Galette, 99
Baked Apples, 104

Asparagus
Roasted Miso Asparagus, 68

Avocado
Avocado Eggs, 19
Avocado Toast, 17
Chicken Empanadas, 27
Spiced Bean Tacos, 70

Bacon
Avocado Toast, 17
Bacon-Wrapped Dates, 97
Bacon Wrapped Potatoes, 50
Bacon Wrapped Sausages, 47
Bacon Wrapped Scallops, 62
Breakfast Bombs, 18
Cheese-Bacon Fries, 85
Crispy Potato Skins, 71
Egg Bacon Cups, 23
Egg Bites, 21
Stuffed Mushrooms, 92

Bananas
Banana Cake, 110
Banana Chips, 95
Bananas, 98

BBQ Sauce
BBQ Chicken Wings, 36
Hamburger, 46

Beans
Spiced Bean Tacos, 70

Beef
Hamburger, 46
Juicy Steak, 48
Meatballs, 52
Super Easy Meatloaf, 54

Bell Pepper
Breaded Jerk Chicken, 38
Chicken Stuffed Peppers, 37
Egg-Bacon Cups, 23
Fried Potato & Sausages, 55
Roasted Vegetables, 78
Stuffed Chicken Breasts, 40
Super Easy Meatloaf, 54

Biscuits
Breakfast Bombs, 18
Chicken Bombs, 29

Blueberries
Blueberry Crisp, 111

Bread
Avocado Eggs, 19
Avocado Toast, 17
Bread Pudding, 105

Cheesy Chicken Sandwich, 13
French Toast Sticks, 14
Monkey Bread, 108
Pizza Bagels, 93

Breadcrumbs
Breaded Chicken Tenders, 35
Breaded Fish Fillets, 66
Catfish Nuggets, 64
Coconut Shrimp, 60
Crispy Fish Cake, 63
Eggplant Parmesan Bites, 72
Fried Calamari, 91
Fried Cheese Sticks, 94
Meatballs, 52
Popcorn Shrimp, 88
Salmon Burger, 59
Super Easy Meatloaf, 54
Tuna Cakes, 65
Turkey Meatballs, 41

Breakfast Sausage
Bacon Wrapped Sausages, 47
Breakfast Burritos, 22

Broccoli
Garlic Broccoli, 82

Brussels sprouts
Roasted Vegetables, 78

Burger Buns
Greek Chicken Burger, 32
Hamburger, 46
Salmon Burger, 59

Buttermilk
Breaded Bone-in Chicken, 45
Catfish Nuggets, 64
Crispy Bone-in Chicken, 42
Fluffy Pancakes, 15
Quick Scones, 101

Butternut Squash
Fried Spaghetti Squash, 84
Roasted Butternut Squash, 81

Cabbage
Cabbage Steak, 75

Calamari
Fried Calamari, 91

Carrot
Carrot Cake, 109
Fried Potato & Sausages, 55
Roasted Vegetables, 78

Catfish
Breaded Fish Fillets, 66
Catfish Nuggets, 64

Cauliflower
Korean Cauliflower Bites, 69

Cheese
Bacon-Wrapped Dates, 97
Breakfast Bombs, 18
Breakfast Burritos, 22

Cheese & Ham Egg Rolls, 16
Cheese-Bacon Fries, 85
Cheesy Chicken Sandwich, 13
Chicken Bombs, 29
Chicken Empanadas, 27
Chicken Stuffed Peppers, 37
Greek Chicken Burger, 32
Green Chicken Enchiladas, 33
Crispy Potato Skins, 71
Egg Bites, 21
Eggplant Parmesan Bites, 72
English Muffin Pizza, 24
Fried Cheese Sticks, 94
Garlic Broccoli, 82
Meatballs, 52
Nachos, 89
Pizza Bagels, 93
Pizza Rolls, 90
Quesadillas, 26
Roasted Tomatoes, 74
Stuffed Chicken Breasts, 40
Stuffed Mushrooms, 92
Super Easy Meatloaf, 54
Tender Pork Chops, 57
Turkey Meatballs, 41
Zucchini Fritters, 83

Chicken
Almond Crusted Chicken, 31
BBQ Chicken Wings, 36
Breaded Chicken Tenders, 35
Breaded Bone-in Chicken, 45
Breaded Jerk Chicken, 38
Cheesy Chicken Sandwich, 13
Chicken Bombs, 29
Chicken Empanadas, 27
Chicken Stuffed Peppers, 37
Crispy Bone-in Chicken, 42
Firecracker Chicken, 28
Flavorful Chicken Breasts, 39
Greek Chicken Burger, 32
Green Chicken Enchiladas, 33
Honey Garlic Wings, 34
Mustard Chicken Wings, 30
Stuffed Chicken Breasts, 40

Clementine
Fried Turkey Crown, 43

Cod
Breaded Fish Fillets, 66
Crispy Fish Cake, 63

Coleslaw
Egg Rolls, 49

Corn
Nachos, 89
Spiced Bean Tacos, 70

Dates
Bacon-Wrapped Dates, 97

Egg
Apple Fritters. 103
Avocado Eggs, 19
Banana Cake, 110
Bread Pudding, 105
Breakfast Bombs, 18

114

Breakfast Burritos, 22
Brownies, 112
Carrot Cake, 109
Catfish Nuggets, 64
Cheese & Ham Egg Rolls, 16
Chicken Empanadas, 27
Coconut Shrimp, 60
Crispy Fish Cake, 63
Cupcakes, 102
Egg Bites, 21
Egg-Bacon Cups, 23
Eggplant Parmesan Bites, 72
Firecracker Chicken, 28
Fluffy Pancakes, 15
French Toast Sticks, 14
Fried Calamari, 91
Fried Cheese Sticks, 94
Hard Boiled Eggs, 20
Meatballs, 52
Nutella Cookies, 106
Popcorn Shrimp, 88
Quick Scones, 101
Super Easy Meatloaf, 54
Tuna Cakes, 65
Zucchini Fritters, 83

Egg Roll Wrappers
Cheese & Ham Egg Rolls, 16
Egg Rolls, 49

Eggplant
Eggplant Parmesan Bites, 72

English Muffins
English Muffin Pizza, 24

Flour
Apple Fritters. 103
Baked Apples, 104
Banana Cake, 110
Blueberry Crisp, 111
Breaded Bone-in Chicken, 45
Brownies, 112
Carrot Cake, 109
Catfish Nuggets, 64
Coconut Shrimp, 60
Crispy Bone-in Chicken, 42
Cupcakes, 102
Easy Donuts, 100
Fluffy Pancakes, 15
Fried Calamari, 91
Fried Cheese Sticks, 94
Korean Cauliflower Bites, 69
Nutella Cookies, 106
Popcorn Shrimp, 88
Quick Scones, 101
Zucchini Fritters, 83

Ham
Cheese & Ham Egg Rolls, 16
Glazed Ham, 53

Heavy Cream
Bread Pudding, 105
Cupcakes, 102
Egg Bites, 21

Honey
Banana Cake, 110
Glazed Ham, 53
Honey Garlic Wings, 34
Korean Cauliflower Bites, 69

Honey Chicken Wings, 30
Roasted Miso Asparagus, 68

Lamb
Roasted Lamb Leg, 51

Mayonnaise
Almond Crusted Chicken, 31
Crispy Fish Cake, 63
Crispy Potato Skins, 71
Mustard Honey Chicken
Wings, 30
Salmon Burger, 59
Tuna Cakes, 65

Milk
Breakfast Burritos, 22
Cupcakes, 102
Egg Bites, 21
French Toast Sticks, 14
Meatballs, 52
Monkey Bread, 108
Quick Scones, 101
Super Easy Meatloaf, 54
Turkey Meatballs, 41

Mushroom
Garlic Mushrooms, 73
Stuffed Mushrooms, 92

Oats
Baked Apples, 104
Blueberry Crisp, 111
Granola, 25

Peaches
Caramelized Peaches, 107

Pepperoni
English Muffin Pizza, 24
Pizza Bagels, 93
Pizza Rolls, 90

Pesto
Chicken Stuffed Peppers, 37

Pie Crust
Apple Galette, 99
Chicken Empanadas, 27

Pork
Egg Rolls, 49
Meatballs, 52
Roast Pork, 56
Tender Pork Chops, 57

Potato
Bacon Wrapped Potatoes, 50
Breaded Jerk Chicken, 38
Breakfast Burritos, 22
Cheese-Bacon Fries, 85
Crispy Potato Skins, 71
Crispy Potato Wedges, 76
Fried Potato & Sausages, 55
Roasted Lamb Leg, 51
Roasted Vegetables, 78
Spicy French Fries, 77

Quinoa
Chicken Stuffed Peppers, 37

Raisins
Granola, 25

Refried Beans
Quesadillas, 26
Salmon
Chimichurri Salmon, 58
Fried Salmon, 61
Salmon Burger, 59

Scallops
Bacon Wrapped Scallops, 62

Shrimp
Coconut Shrimp, 60
Popcorn Shrimp, 88
Sour Cream
Cheese-Bacon Fries, 85
Chicken Bombs, 29
Chicken Empanadas, 27
Crispy Potato Skins, 71

Soy Sauce
Crispy Tofu, 79
Egg Rolls, 49
Garlic Mushrooms, 73
Honey Garlic Wings, 34
Korean Cauliflower Bites, 69

Spinach
Greek Chicken Burger, 32
Stuffed Chicken Breasts, 40

Tilapia
Breaded Fish Fillets, 66
White Fish with Garlic, 67

Tofu
Crispy Tofu, 79

Tomato
Avocado Toast, 17
Greek Chicken Burger, 32
Nachos, 89
Roasted Tomatoes, 74
Spiced Bean Tacos, 70

Tomato Paste
Super Easy Meatloaf, 54

Tortillas
Breakfast Burritos, 22
Green Chicken Enchiladas, 33
Nachos, 89
Quesadillas, 26
Spiced Bean Tacos, 70

Tuna
Tuna Cakes, 65

Turkey
Fried Turkey Crown, 43
Roasted Turkey Legs, 44
Turkey Meatballs, 41

Walnuts
Carrot Cake, 109
Granola, 25

Zucchini
Breaded Jerk Chicken, 38
Zucchini Fritters, 83

Made in the USA
Las Vegas, NV
21 December 2023

83294009R00066